REVV UP WITH KRSNA

SHORT STORIES TO INSPIRE YOUNG MINDS: TIMELESS LESSONS FROM THE BHAGAVAD GITA

MEIRA

To Reyansh

Your boundless love for reading and your infectious zest for life have been a constant source of inspiration to me. Watching you grow has been a joy beyond words. May you continue to blossom from the smart, curious boy you are today into an extraordinary human being who touches the world with wisdom, kindness, and courage.

Contents

Foreword

The Bhagavad Gita, often revered as the song of divine wisdom, has been a guiding light for millions over the centuries. It's timeless teachings, encompassing profound insights on life, duty, self discipline and inner strength hold the power to transform and inspire every individual who opens their heart to it. It has been a source of inspiration for people of all ages.

Preface

Today, children and teenagers are growing up in a world dominated by social media and an endless cycle of comparisons. Many find themselves trapped in a web of unrealistic expectations, leading to anxiety and depression. In some heartbreaking instances despair pushes them to take drastic steps. The constant need for validation and the pressures of modern life can make young minds feel overwhelmed and lost. It is in these moments that the teachings of the Gita become a vital lifeline—a manual for life that offers clarity, strength, and peace. But how do we make it's teachings accessible to young minds—children and teenagers who are still discovering their path in life?

This book was born from that very thought. In crafting this book, I have drawn upon my love for storytelling and my passion for making profound ideas accessible to all. I have tried to illustrate the Gita's teachings through relatable stories, and simple explanations, ensuring that it's wisdom feels both approachable and meaningful. My hope is that young readers will see the Gita not as a distant scripture but as a friendly guide—one that speaks directly to their hearts and helps them navigate the joys and challenges of growing up. Each story reflects a teaching from the Gita, simplified and woven into narratives that capture emotions, dilemmas, and triumphs.

I hope that this book doesn't just tell stories but sparks reflection. That it makes young readers think about their own decisions, their struggles, and their dreams & that it inspires them to see life through the lens of wisdom, responsibility, and purpose.

To the parents, educators, and mentors who might share this book with the younger generation, I invite you to read alongside them, to spark discussions and reflections, and to make this a shared journey of discovery.

Discover the magic of the Gita and let its wisdom guide you to a life of balance, resilience, and happiness. This book is your invitation to embrace life's challenges with an open heart and a curious mind.

This book is not meant to be read in one sitting and put away. Instead, it is a companion—something to return to whenever there is a need for guidance, clarity, or simply a good story. May these tales ignite curiosity and help young minds find their own path, with the Gita as their silent mentor.

With gratitude and hope,
MEIRA

Acknowledgements

This book is a labour of love, born from the desire to make the timeless wisdom of the Bhagavad Gita accessible and engaging for young minds. As I reflect on this journey, there are several people and sources of inspiration without whom this book would not have been possible.

First and foremost, my deepest love goes out to Sohom and Reyansh - both of them has been the greatest gift from God. As they navigate life's journey, I wanted to gift them something precious —I wanted to give them wisdom they could cherish and carry with them always. Through these narratives, I hope they find guidance, strength, and the timeless teachings of the Gita woven into lessons they can live by. **This book is my way of holding their hands, even when I'm not around, and whispering to them the values that will light their path.**

I would also like to express my deep appreciation to the book 'Bhagavad Gita As It Is' by His Divine Grace A.C Bhaktivendanta Swami Prabhupada, from which I have drawn the translations of the shlokas featured in this book. The clarity and authenticity of this revered text have been instrumental in shaping the lessons shared here.

A special note of gratitude goes to my Guru, whose guidance has been invaluable in deepening my understanding of the Bhagavad Gita's teachings. The courses I attended on Bhagavad Gita opened my mind to the profound wisdom hidden within it's verses, allowing me to interpret and present these lessons in a way that resonates with young readers. Their teachings have been my compass, and I am forever indebted to them.

I would also like to thank all the readers who will embark on this journey through these stories. May these pages inspire, guide, and spark a love for the eternal wisdom of the Bhagavad Gita within you.

Prologue

This collection of 20 short stories are woven around lessons from the Bhagavad Gita, presented in a way that speaks directly to the heart of a young soul. Whether it's about overcoming fear, learning the power of focus, embracing change, or understanding one's duties in the world—these stories aim to show that the path to wisdom is not a distant one, but one that is within our reach, every single day.

As you flip through these pages, you will find that the teachings of the Gita aren't just ancient knowledge meant for scholars or philosophers. They are lessons meant for you, for the world we live in today. These stories may not just entertain you, but they might also inspire you to think, reflect, and grow.

The characters you will meet in these stories might be similar to someone you know—or even yourself. They will struggle with doubts, face challenges, and seek answers. But in the end, they will find their way, guided by the ageless wisdom of the Gita.

This book is a journey. A journey of self-discovery, learning, and growth. So, as you embark on this journey, remember: the teachings of the Gita are not just for the pages of a book. They are for the heart, the mind, and the soul.

May its timeless wisdom inspire you to see life's challenges as opportunities, to recognize the strength within you, and to find joy and meaning in every step of your journey. Gita teaches us—no matter who we are or where we come from—we all have the power to become the best version of ourselves.

Let's walk this path together.

CHAPTER ONE

The Painting Competition

It was a bright sunny morning, and Arya sat at her desk, staring at the blank canvas as though it might give her answers. The annual school painting competition was only a week away, and Arya's mind was a whirlwind of worry since she had no idea what to paint.

Her best friend, Anaya, had already finalized her masterpiece—a breathtaking scene of mountains, rivers, and a glowing sunrise. Arya, on the other hand, was stuck in a spiral of self-doubt.

Her mom walked in with a plate of freshly cut apples and peanut butter. "Arya, you've been sitting here all morning. What's bothering you?" she said, placing a hand on Arya's shoulder.

Arya groaned, burying her face in her arms. "Mom, I don't know what to paint. Anaya's painting is going to be amazing. She's so talented, and I... I don't think I can even compete with her. What if I can't do something as good as hers? What if I fail? What if everyone laughs at me?"

Mom sat down beside her and smiled. "Arya, let me tell you something. Have you ever seen a gardener planting flowers?"

Arya nodded, curious where this was going.

"The gardener plants seeds, waters them every day, and takes care of the soil. But can the gardener control when the flowers will bloom or how beautiful they will be?"

Arya thought for a moment. "No, I guess not."

"Exactly," Mom said, her voice warm and soothing. "The gardener's job is to take care of the plants. The rest is up to nature. It's the same with your painting. Your job is to paint with all your heart. Whether you win or lose isn't in your control. But how much effort and love you put into your work—that's entirely up to you."

Arya frowned, still not convinced. "But what's the point if I don't win? It'll feel like all my hard work was wasted."

Mom laughed gently and ruffled Arya's hair. "Why don't you start painting and find out? Focus on what you love about painting. Winning is nice, but it's not the reason you started, is it?"

Arya sighed, but something in her mom's words stayed with her. That evening, she pulled out her paints and thought deeply about what made her happiest. She remembered the summers she spent under the giant banyan tree near her grandmother's house—the cool shade, the chirping birds, and the laughter of cousins playing.

With each stroke of her brush, Arya began to lose herself in the memory. Day by day, her painting started coming to life. The more she painted, the less she thought about the competition. Instead, she began enjoying the process—choosing colors, adding tiny details, and remembering the happy times she spent at her grandma's home. The leaves of the banyan tree came alive on the canvas, the roots stretching like arms of an old friend. The more she painted, the less she worried about the competition.

By the end of the week, Arya had created a vivid, heartfelt painting that captured her favorite childhood memory

On the day of the competition, Arya walked into the school auditorium, carrying her painting nervously. She glanced at Anaya's work—it was stunning, just as she had imagined. The mountains perfectly shaded and looked alive, and the sunrise glowing vibrantly just like fire.

"Wow, Anaya's painting is incredible," Arya muttered under her breath.

Her mom, who had come to support her, whispered, "Arya, remember what I said? Focus on what you've created, not what others have done."

Taking a deep breath, Arya set up her painting.

As the judges walked around, Arya felt her heart race. When the winner was announced, she wasn't surprised—it was Anaya. The auditorium erupted in applause, and Anaya beamed as she accepted her trophy. Arya clapped too, but she couldn't ignore the lump in her throat.

After the ceremony, one of the judges approached Arya. "You're Arya, right?"

"Y-Yes," she stammered.

The judge smiled warmly. "I loved your painting. It reminded me of my childhood summers spent at my grandmother's house. It may not have won today, but it's a truly special piece of art. It felt so personal and full of emotion. "

Arya's eyes widened. "Really? You liked it?"

"Absolutely," the judge said. "Winning isn't everything. The passion and emotion you put into your painting make it unforgettable."

As Arya walked home with her mom, she felt lighter, happier. Arya felt a warm glow inside "Mom, you were right," she said. "Painting this made me really happy. Winning would have been an icing on the cake but I think I've already won in my own way."Mom smiled and said, "That's the spirit, Arya. Life isn't about the trophies—it's about how much joy and meaning you bring to what you do."

Life lesson: Focus on your efforts, not the outcome.

Just like Arya, focus on giving your best effort and enjoying the process of whatever you do. The outcome is beyond your control, but the dedication and love you pour into your actions will make your journey worthwhile.

Bhagavad Gita Shloka :
*'karmany evadhikaras te ma phalesu kadacana
ma karma-phala-hetur bhur ma te sango stv akarmani'*
(Chapter 2, Verse 47)

Translation – 'You have a right to perform your prescribed duty, but you are not entitled to the fruits of action. Never consider yourself the cause of the results of your activities and never be attached to not doing your duty.'

Takeaway - Krishna explained to Arjuna that the key to life is focusing on doing your duty without being consumed by the results. He told Arjuna, *"As a warrior, your responsibility is to fight this battle with courage. If you back away, it won't just bring dishonor to you but will also create disorder in society."*

Now, think about your life as a student. Your battlefield isn't Kurukshetra, and your duty isn't wielding a sword—**it's learning, growing, and giving your best effort**. Your job is to attend classes, complete assignments, and study with sincerity. But if you constantly stress about grades or compare yourself to others, you'll end up feeling just as lost and doubtful as Arjuna did on the battlefield.

Krishna also reminded Arjuna that **results are never fully in our control**—they depend on many factors, like timing, effort, and even luck. That's why instead of chasing trophies or worrying about applause, you should focus on the **process of learning**. When you put in sincere effort, stay committed to your goals, and keep improving—**you've already succeeded**.

True success isn't just about getting the best marks; it's about **building character, staying dedicated, and never giving up**. And when you embrace this mindset, you become stronger—one step at a time. Just like Arjuna found his strength through Krishna's wisdom, you, too, can find yours by focusing on what truly matters.

• 5 •

The Unseen Enemy

Amit sat on the park bench, staring blankly at the ground as the evening breeze rustled the leaves around him. His school bag lay forgotten by his side. Thoughts swirled in his mind—thoughts of all the times he had failed a math test, stumbled during a sports match, or felt invisible in a crowd.

"I can't do anything right," Amit muttered to himself. "Why do I even try? Everyone else is so much better than me."

Just then, his friend Maya jogged over, panting from her evening run. She noticed Amit's slouched shoulders and the look of defeat on his face.

"Hey, Amit, what's up? You look like the weight of the world is on your shoulders," Maya said, sitting beside him.

Amit sighed deeply. "I don't know, Maya. I feel like I'm my own worst enemy. No matter how hard I try, this voice in my head keeps saying, 'You're not good enough,' or 'You're going to fail again.' It's exhausting."

Maya tilted her head thoughtfully , smiled and said. "You know, Amit, your mind is a bit like a wild animal."

Amit raised an eyebrow. "A wild animal?"

"Yes," Maya said with a small smile. "Imagine a wild tiger roaming free. If it's left untrained, it can wreak havoc, right? But if a skilled trainer teaches it discipline, that same tiger can perform incredible feats and become an ally."

Amit frowned, trying to process the analogy. "So... are you saying my mind is like a wild tiger?"

"Exactly," Maya said. "When you let negative thoughts run loose, they control you, and you end up feeling powerless. But if you train your mind to focus on the positive and shut out the negative, it can help you achieve amazing things."

"But how do I even begin to train my mind?" Amit asked, leaning forward, intrigued

Maya grinned. "Start by being aware of what your mind is saying. When you catch yourself thinking something like, 'I can't do this,' stop and challenge that thought. Instead, say, 'I will try my best.' It's like teaching the tiger to respond to your commands. Over time, the more you practice, the easier it becomes.".

Amit leaned back, letting the idea sink in. "So... it's like turning my mind from an enemy into a friend?"

"Exactly," Maya said, patting his shoulder. "A well-trained mind becomes your greatest ally. It'll push you to keep going when things get tough and remind you of your strengths when you're doubting yourself."

That night, Amit decided to give Maya's advice a shot. As he sat down to study for his upcoming math test, the familiar voice in his head whispered, "You're going to fail again. Why even bother?"

Amit paused, took a deep breath, and said out loud, "No, I'm not going to fail. I'm going to give it my best shot. Even if I don't ace it, I'll learn and get better."

It felt strange at first, but Amit noticed something surprising—just saying those words made him feel a little more confident.

Over the next few weeks, Amit practiced replacing his negative thoughts with positive ones. Amit kept practicing this simple technique, and over time, his negative thoughts became less frequent, and his mind started to feel like a friend—supporting him in his goals and ambitions.

When he stumbled during a sports match, instead of thinking, "I'm terrible at this," he told himself, "I'll practice harder and get better." When he got a low grade, instead of feeling hopeless, he thought, "This is a chance to improve. I'll ask my teacher for help."

Gradually, Amit began to notice a change. The voice in his head became less critical, and he started to feel more capable and optimistic.

A month later, Amit stood on the stage during the school assembly. He had been asked to share his thoughts on overcoming challenges, and for the first time in his life, he didn't feel nervous.

"Everyone faces doubts and fears," Amit began, looking out at his classmates. "For the longest time, I thought my mind was my enemy, constantly reminding me of my failures. But a friend taught me something important—that my mind is like a wild animal. If I let it run wild, it'll hurt me. But if I train it, it can help me achieve anything."

As Amit stepped down from the stage, Maya, sitting in the front row, gave him a big thumbs-up. His classmates surrounded him, clapping and cheering. Some of them even shared their own struggles with self-doubt. For the first time, Amit realized that he wasn't alone in his journey—everyone faced their own inner battles.

Walking home that evening, Amit felt lighter, as though a heavy weight had been lifted off his shoulders. He thought back to Maya's analogy about the wild tiger.

"Train your thoughts, and you'll train your future," he whispered to himself.

The words felt powerful now, not just like advice but like a truth he had lived. Amit understood that while he couldn't control what life threw at him, he could always control how he responded. His mind was no longer an enemy but a loyal friend, ready to help him face challenges and find joy in the journey.That night, as he lay in bed, Amit smiled to himself. Life wasn't perfect, but he no longer felt afraid. He was ready for the next adventure, knowing he had the strength to handle whatever came his way—one thought at a time.

Life lesson: Control your mind.

A disciplined mind is a powerful ally that can guide you toward success and happiness. However, if left uncontrolled, it can become your greatest enemy, filling your life with doubt and fear. Train your thoughts, and you'll train your future.

Bhagavad Gita Shloka :
'bandhur atmatmanas tasya yenatmaivatmana jitah
anatmanas tu satrutve vartetatmaiva satru-vat'
(Chapter 6, Verse 6)

Translation – 'For him who has conquered the mind, the mind is the best of friends; but for one who has failed to do so, his mind will remain the greatest enemy.'

Takeaway - Krishna teaches us that **your mind can be your biggest cheerleader or your greatest roadblock**—it all depends on how you train it. Imagine your mind as a super-fast sports car. If you take control of the steering wheel, focus on the road, and drive with confidence, it will take you exactly where you want to go—toward success, happiness, and your dreams. But if you let the car run wild, distracted and out of control, it might crash into obstacles and leave you stuck.

A disciplined mind is like a skilled driver—it knows where to go and how to navigate challenges. It helps you stay focused in class, push through tough exams, and stay motivated even when things get hard. But when your mind is filled with fear, self-doubt, anger, or distractions, it's like getting lost on a road with no map—you keep going in circles and never reach your destination.

Krishna also warns us about letting unchecked emotions like greed, jealousy, and anger take control. Think of these as potholes on your journey. If you keep falling into them, your ride becomes bumpy and frustrating. But if you learn to spot them early, slow down, and steer around them with self-control, your journey will be smooth and fulfilling.

Managing your mind isn't always easy, but it's the secret to success, confidence, and a life full of purpose. So, ask yourself—**are you driving your mind, or is your mind driving you? The choice is yours!**

CHAPTER THREE

The Two Wolves

An old army chief was sitting by a fire with his grandson. The flames crackled softly as the boy gazed into the fire, looking troubled. Noticing his grandson's discomfort, the old man asked, "What's on your mind?"

The boy sighed and said, "Grandfather, I feel like there's a war inside me. Sometimes, I feel brave and confident, like I can achieve anything. But other times, I'm filled with fear and doubt. Why is it so hard to stay positive?"

The old man smiled gently and said, "Ah, my boy, that's because inside every person, two wolves are always fighting. One wolf is full of fear, doubt, and failure. It whispers to you that you're not good enough, that you'll never succeed. The other wolf is full of belief, confidence, and courage. It encourages you, telling you to trust yourself and keep going."

The boy looked concerned. "Which wolf wins, Grandfather?"

The old man paused, poking the fire thoughtfully with a stick. Then he said, "The one you feed, my child. If you listen to the wolf of fear and give it your attention, it will grow stronger. But if you feed the wolf of confidence with positive thoughts and belief in yourself, it will overpower the other."

The boy lay in his bed that night, staring up at the ceiling, thinking about his grandfather's words. His Grandfather says "Wisdom often came in quiet moments". As he drifted into sleep, he found his mind racing with thoughts. It wasn't just about his fears and doubts anymore; it was about the choices he had to make, every day, in how he saw himself.

The next morning, he woke up early, just before the sun had fully risen. His grandfather was already awake, sitting on a nearby rock with a steaming mug of tea. The boy walked over to him, still wrapped in his blanket. "Grandfather," he said softly, "I've been thinking a lot about the two wolves inside of me."

The old man looked up with a twinkle in his eye. "And what have you decided, my boy?"

"I want to feed the wolf of confidence," the boy said, determination in his voice. "But sometimes, the other wolf—of fear and doubt—comes up so suddenly. I don't know what to do when it's so strong."

The old man nodded, his face thoughtful. "It's true, the wolf of fear can be loud. But there's something you must remember: the wolf of belief doesn't always roar. It speaks quietly, like a whisper. And that's the key—when fear rises, you must listen more closely to that quiet voice of confidence."

They sat together in silence for a moment, the boy contemplating. His grandfather stood and gestured to the woods around them. "Come," he said. "I will show you something."

They walked into the forest, where the morning mist still clung to the trees. The old man stopped by a large oak tree and pointed to a small patch of ground covered in moss. "Look closely at this place," he said. "Do you see how the moss grows only where the sunlight touches?"

The boy knelt down and looked closely. "Yes," he said, "the moss grows only in the light."

"Exactly," the old man said. "And so it is with your mind. The wolf you feed is like the sunlight. If you feed it with thoughts of fear, you'll find yourself in the shadows. But if you feed it with belief and positive thoughts, you allow the light of courage and confidence to shine. That is how you grow stronger."

The boy's eyes brightened with understanding. He realized that it wasn't enough to simply choose confidence over fear—it was about making sure the confidence had room to grow by clearing out the space for it, just as sunlight makes the moss thrive.

Over the following weeks, the boy practiced this new way of thinking. When doubt crept in, he would take a deep breath and remind himself of the quiet voice of belief his grandfather had spoken of. Slowly but surely, he began to see changes in himself. As the months passed, the boy's confidence continued to grow. He learned to feed the wolf of belief, even when his fears tried to rise up like shadows in the corners of his mind. The more he practiced, the more he saw the changes not just in himself, but in the way others treated him. The quiet strength he had discovered began to shine through in his words and actions.

One day, as the boy and his grandfather were working together in the fields, the old man spoke. "You've done well, my boy. You've learned to quiet the wolf of fear and listen to the wolf of confidence. But remember this: feeding the wolf of belief is not a one-time choice. It's a practice, a lifelong journey. There will be moments in your life when the wolves will battle fiercely, and you'll feel torn between them. The important thing is to never stop choosing the wolf of belief, even when it's hard."

The boy nodded, taking his grandfather's words to heart. He understood now that the battle wasn't something that would go away—it was something he would face for the rest of his life. But he also knew that each time he chose the path of belief, he would grow stronger.

Soon, news came to the village that there would be a grand competition—a test of strength, skill, and courage. The boy's heart raced as he heard the stories of past champions. Some were warriors, others skilled craftsmen, and many were much older than him. A voice of doubt crept into his mind. *What if I'm not good enough?* The wolf of fear stirred within him.

That night, as he sat by the fire, he felt the familiar unease. His grandfather noticed, his eyes wise and kind. "What is troubling you, my boy?"

"I want to enter the competition, Grandfather," the boy said, "but I'm afraid I won't be able to do it. There are so many strong people who will compete."

The old man smiled gently, "Do you remember what I told you about the wolves? Fear will always try to make you doubt yourself, but you must listen to the wolf of confidence. That voice, though quiet, is the one that will guide you. Success doesn't always mean winning, my boy. Sometimes, it's about having the courage to try, even when the odds are against you."

The boy nodded, his mind racing. He knew that his grandfather was right. The wolf of belief would be his guide, and his journey was about pushing through his doubts and fears, no matter the outcome.

The day of the competition arrived, and the village was filled with excitement. People from nearby towns gathered to watch. The boy's heart pounded in his chest as he stood among the competitors, most of whom were much older and stronger than he was. The wolf of fear whispered, *You won't win. You'll embarrass yourself. Just walk away now.* But then, the quiet voice of belief rose above the noise. *You've trained for this. You're stronger than you know. Do your best, and that is enough.*

The boy took a deep breath and stepped forward, ready to face whatever challenges lay ahead.

The competition was fierce, and the tasks were difficult. There were races, puzzles, and feats of strength. At one point, the boy had to carry a heavy load up a steep hill, and his legs trembled with exhaustion. The wolf of fear urged him to give up. *You can't do this. It's too hard.*

But the wolf of belief kept pushing him forward. *You are capable. Trust yourself. Keep going.*

With each step, the boy drew strength from within. His muscles burned, but his resolve was stronger. He reached the top, breathless but victorious, and continued through the challenges with a new sense of determination.

Finally, the last challenge was before him: a test of courage. The competitors had to face their fears in front of the crowd. A giant, dark maze stood before them, and they had to find their way out. The walls of the maze seemed to close in, and the air was thick with tension. Fear crept up on the boy again, but he stood firm. *This is the moment where the wolf of belief must take control,* he thought.

He entered the maze, the darkness pressing around him. His mind raced with doubt, but the quiet voice of belief guided him forward. "You've faced worse before," it whispered. "You've overcome more than this." Each step through the maze felt like a battle, but he remembered the lessons his grandfather had taught him: *The wolf of belief is with you, always. Trust yourself and take the next step.*

Finally, after what felt like an eternity, he emerged from the maze, breathless but triumphant. The crowd cheered, and the boy smiled, not because he had won the competition, but because he had faced his fears and chosen the path of courage.

Later that night, as he sat by the fire with his grandfather, the old man said, "You did well, my boy. But remember, the greatest victory is not in defeating others, but in overcoming the battle within yourself."From that day on, the boy knew that his true strength didn't come from his victories, but from his ability to choose belief over fear, again and again. And he carried that wisdom with him throughout his life, teaching others that the battle within was the one that mattered most.

<u>*Life lesson: Your beliefs shape who you become.*</u>

The power of belief lies within each of us. True strength comes from the choice to face your fears and doubts with courage and belief. By nurturing it with positive thoughts and actions, we can overcome the challenges. The wolf you choose to feed shapes the person you become. Choose to nurture belief in yourself, and it will guide you to success.

❧❧❧

Bhagavad Gita Shloka :
_'uddhared atmanatmanam natmanam avasadayet
atmaiva hy atmano bandhur atmaiva ripur atmanah'_
(Chapter 6, Verse 5)

❧❧❧

Translation – 'One must deliver himself with the help of his mind, and not degrade himself. The mind is the friend of the conditioned soul and his enemy as well.'

❧❧❧

Takeaway - Krishna teaches us that **what we believe about ourselves shapes who we become.** He told Arjuna, "If you believe you can win this war, you will succeed. But if you let doubt take over, failure is certain." And guess what? **The same is true for you!**

Believing in yourself is like unlocking a superpower. When you trust your abilities, you face challenges head-on, push past fear, and do things you never thought possible. **Your belief fuels your courage**—it's the invisible force that keeps you moving forward, even when things get tough.

Krishna also reminds us that **our beliefs shape our thoughts, and our thoughts guide our actions.** Imagine your mind as a garden—if you plant seeds of confidence, effort, and positivity, you'll grow into a strong, successful person. But if you let negativity and doubt take over, weeds of fear and laziness will slow you down.

Sure, controlling your mind can sometimes feel like taming a wild monkey—it jumps from one thought to another! But with practice, focus, and the right mindset, you can train it. Think of it as programming your inner superhero! Feed your mind with positive, powerful thoughts, and you'll unlock hidden strengths, tackle obstacles like a warrior, and set yourself on the path to success, happiness, and greatness.

So, what do you choose to believe? Your belief is where your power begins!

The Busy Bee

Nina often felt overwhelmed by the numerous tasks she had to do in a day/ One day, she expressed her frustration to her Aunt Maya.

"Aunt Maya, I just don't know where to start! I feel likc I'm constantly moving but never accomplishing anything," Nina said.

Aunt Maya smiled and said, "Do you see the bee buzzing around in the garden? The bee is always busy, moving from one flower to the next, gathering nectar. It never stops, and yet, it is always working toward its goal. Just like that, action is a part of life. You can never stop—it's in your nature. The key is to direct your energy toward meaningful tasks. Try to organize and prioritize your work instead of rushing through the day. Wake up early and collect your thoughts on the tasks in hand. Decide on your TO DO list and work on them one at a time."

As weeks went by, Nina decided to listen to her aunt's advice. Each morning, Nina set her alarm a little earlier than usual. The soft chime of the clock seemed to greet her gently, and instead of hitting snooze, she stretched and sat up. Her mornings began to transform in a way she never imagined possible. The hectic rush of getting ready for school and racing through chores had always left her feeling frazzled, as if she were running behind even before the day began. But now, she had a new routine, one that brought a sense of clarity and calm.

One evening, Nina found herself sitting at the kitchen table, her homework spread out in front of her. For the first time in a while, she felt in control. "Focus on one thing at a time," she would remind herself, just as Aunt Maya had taught her. The sense of purpose in her list helped her approach her tasks with a new perspective. Instead of feeling overwhelmed by everything she had to do, she found that taking a moment to organize and prioritize gave her a feeling of control. As she worked through her assignments, she couldn't help but smile at how much easier everything felt. She was no longer overwhelmed by the sheer volume of her to-do list. She was simply moving from one task to the next, just like the bee.

Just then, Aunt Maya walked into the room and sat down across from Nina. She noticed the peace in Nina's expression and the way she was focused on her homework. Aunt Maya noticed the change in Nina. One morning, as Nina was folding laundry, Aunt Maya remarked, "I've seen such a difference in you lately, Nina. You seem so much more present."

"You've really been doing well, haven't you?" Aunt Maya said with a proud smile.

Nina nodded, putting down her pencil for a moment to reflect. "I feel like I'm finally getting the hang of it, Aunt Maya. I used to rush through everything, but now it's different. I'm taking things one step at a time, and I'm not rushing to get to the end. I'm enjoying the process."

Aunt Maya smiled warmly. "That's wonderful to hear, my dear. You know, you're not just learning how to manage tasks—you're learning the art of presence. The bee doesn't hurry, it simply does its work with intention, and it's in the doing that it finds its purpose."

Nina thought about this. "So it's not just about finishing the work, but about being in the moment while I'm doing it?"

"Exactly," Aunt Maya said. "When you're fully present in what you're doing, whether it's schoolwork, chores, or even just having a conversation, you give yourself the space to truly engage. And when you do that, not only does the task become easier, but you also find a deeper satisfaction in it."

Nina paused for a moment, considering her aunt's words. She realized how true it was. In the past, she had rushed through everything, hoping to get it all done quickly. But now, she noticed how much more fulfilling each moment felt. Even washing the dishes, something she had always dreaded, was becoming a task she could enjoy. The warm water, the sound of plates clinking, and the rhythm of scrubbing—everything felt more peaceful when she wasn't rushing to finish.

As Nina spent more time reflecting on the lessons she'd learned, she started to notice the small things around her more. She found joy in the little moments—the way the sunlight filtered through the window in the morning, the sound of the birds outside, or the way the flowers bloomed in the garden. Each moment felt full of potential, just like the bees that buzzed from flower to flower, never hurrying, but always purposeful.

One day, while Aunt Maya was gardening, Nina decided to join her. She had been helping out more around the house lately, but she hadn't spent much time with her aunt outdoors. As they worked side by side, planting new flowers and tending to the garden, Nina felt a deep sense of peace.

"I've learned a lot from you, Aunt Maya," Nina said, digging her hands into the soil. "I never realized how much can be accomplished just by focusing on what's in front of me."

Aunt Maya smiled, her hands busy planting seeds. "That's the beauty of life, Nina. We often look so far ahead, always thinking about the next thing, that we miss what's right in front of us. The bee doesn't worry about the future. It simply does its work and trusts that it's making a difference, even if it can't see the whole picture."

Nina thought about that. She had always been a planner, thinking about what she needed to do next, but now she was starting to realize that the beauty was in the present moment. The garden, the bees, the tasks she did each day—they all had a purpose, even if they weren't immediately apparent.

That evening, Nina went to bed with a sense of calm she hadn't felt in a long time. The house was tidied, her homework completed, and her heart full of gratitude for the lessons she had learned. As she drifted to sleep, she felt a quiet confidence in her ability to face the day ahead—just as the bee does, moving with purpose and intention, one step at a time.

The next morning, Nina woke up with the same sense of peace. She made her bed, prepared breakfast, and tackled her tasks without rushing. She had learned that life wasn't about checking things off a list or speeding through to the end. It was about the journey, the process, and being fully present in each moment.From that day on, Nina made a habit of organizing her day with intention, much like the bee. She no longer felt like she was running in circles, overwhelmed by the endless to-do list. Instead, she felt empowered, knowing that every small action brought her one step closer to her goals. As Nina moved forward with this new mindset, she found that everything seemed a little easier, a little brighter, and a lot more meaningful.

Life lesson: Take action.

Like the busy bee, we can achieve great things when we focus our energy on meaningful tasks. By taking action step by step, we can accomplish our goals without feeling overwhelmed. We should channel our energy wisely, taking small steps toward our goals.

Bhagavad Gita Shloka :
'na hi kascit ksanam api jatu tisthaty akarma-krt
karyate hy avasah karma sarvah prakrti-jair gunaih'
(Chapter 3, Verse 5)

Translation – 'Everyone is forced to act helplessly according to the qualities he has acquired from the modes of material nature ; therefore no one can refrain from doing something, not even for a moment.'

Takeaway - Krishna teaches us that action is a natural part of being human—nobody can sit completely idle, even for a moment. It's like we all have a hidden motor inside us that keeps running, pushing us to do something. But here's the real question: **Are you using that energy to build something great or letting it go to waste?**

Think of life like cleaning your messy room. If you just sit around and wish it would magically clean itself, what happens? Nothing! In fact, the mess only gets worse. But the moment you take action—picking up clothes, arranging books, and putting things in place—you create a clean, happy space. Life works exactly the same way!

If you sit back and do nothing, problems and challenges pile up like a messy room. But when you take charge, put in effort, and work toward your goals, you start shaping your dream life—one small step at a time.

Waiting for good things to magically happen? Not gonna work. But if you roll up your sleeves and make things happen, there's no limit to what you can achieve. Your success isn't about luck or miracles—it's about effort, determination, and action.

So, what will you do today? Sit back and let life happen, or take action and create something amazing?

CHAPTER FIVE

Arjuna and the Eye of the Bird

One day, Guru Dronacharya decided to test the focus of his students by arranging an archery competition. He placed a wooden bird high on a tree branch and announced, "Your target is the eye of the bird. Prepare to shoot."

The students lined up eagerly, their bows and arrows ready. The first student was Yudhishthira, Arjuna's elder brother. As he drew his bowstring, Dronacharya asked, "What do you see?"
Yudhishthira replied, "I see the tree, the bird, its feathers, and the branches." Dronacharya shook his head, "You're not ready. Step back."

Next came Bhima. When asked the same question, Bhima said, "I see the bird and the tree." Again, Dronacharya dismissed him.

Finally, it was Arjuna's turn. As he positioned his bow, Dronacharya asked, "What do you see?" Without hesitation, Arjuna said, "I see only the eye of the bird."
Dronacharya smiled, "Shoot." The arrow flew straight and hit the bird's eye with precision.

Dronacharya then addressed the group: "This is the power of focus. Arjuna succeeded because his attention was unwavering. If your mind wanders, your actions lose their direction."

After the archery competition, Guru Dronacharya gathered his students around, allowing them a moment to reflect on the test they had just witnessed. The students were amazed by Arjuna's perfect shot, but they couldn't fully grasp the deeper lesson that had been taught. Their eyes were wide with admiration, but their minds still wandered.

Dronacharya, sensing their confusion, spoke again. "Arjuna's success was not just due to his skill with the bow. His focus was unwavering, his mind completely locked onto the target. Let me explain."

He motioned for the students to sit. "In life, distractions are everywhere—like the tree, the branches, and the bird's feathers that Yudhishthira and Bhima saw. These are all the worries, temptations, and doubts that cloud our vision. They pull us in different directions. But Arjuna didn't see any of that. He saw only the eye of the bird, and in doing so, he allowed everything else to fade away."

The students listened intently, eager to understand.

Dronacharya continued, "When you focus on something with absolute clarity, your mind becomes powerful. You do not waste energy on distractions, and your actions become precise. The world may be full of noise and chaos, but your ability to block it out and direct your energy toward your goal determines your success."

As the students reflected on this, Arjuna remained quiet, his thoughts deep. He had always been trained to focus, but hearing his teacher's explanation made him realize the true depth of the lesson. It wasn't just about archery or martial arts—it was about life itself.

Later that evening, as Arjuna sat alone by the river, he thought about the competition. He could still vividly remember how he had blocked out everything—the rustling of the leaves, the chirping of the birds, and even the other students around him. All he saw was the bird's eye, and the arrow had found its mark effortlessly.

He thought to himself, *This is how I must live my life—ignoring distractions, focusing on my true goals, and not letting anything veer me off course.* He realized that the true challenge of life was not the external obstacles, but the internal ones—the doubts, fears, and distractions that cloud the mind.

The next day, as he prepared for his daily training, Arjuna made a new resolution. He would apply the same level of focus not only in archery but in everything he did. Whether it was studying, practicing his swordsmanship, or helping his brothers, he would stay completely focused on the task at hand.

As the weeks passed, Arjuna noticed a change. His ability to concentrate had grown stronger. His skills in archery sharpened, but so did his wisdom. He understood that the mind, like a bowstring, could only shoot true when it was taut with concentration. Anything less would result in a stray arrow, missing its target.

One day, when his brothers asked him how he could maintain such a level of focus, Arjuna smiled and told them the story of the bird's eye. "You see," he said, "it's not just about physical strength. The true strength lies in the mind. When you direct it with purpose, you can achieve anything."

Yudhishthira, who had struggled with distractions, reflected deeply on Arjuna's words. "I've always been worried about the bigger picture—about all the things I need to do. But I understand now. I need to focus on the task in front of me, not get lost in everything else."

Bhima, with his usual enthusiasm, nodded. "I've always been eager to act quickly, but now I see that patience and focus are just as important as strength."

And so, over time, the brothers learned from Arjuna's example. The power of focus became a lesson they carried with them in every endeavor, whether it was battle, study, or even their relationships with others.Guru Dronacharya, observing their growth, was pleased. He knew that true mastery came not just from skill or strength, but from the ability to focus the mind. And Arjuna had already proven that he possessed that rare ability, making him a master not only of archery but of life itself.

Life lesson: Focus on your goals not on distractions.

Life is full of distractions, and the world will always try to pull your attention in many directions. To achieve your goals, you must learn to focus your energy with clarity and purpose, ignoring the noise around you, just as Arjuna focused on the bird's eye, ignoring everything else.

Bhagavad Gita Shloka :
'vyavasayatmika buddhir ekeha kuru-nandana
bahu-sakha hy anantas ca buddhayo vyavasayinam'
(Chapter 2, Verse 41)

Translation – 'Those who are on this path are resolute in purpose, and their aim is one. O beloved child of the Kurus, the intelligence of those who are irresolute is many branched.'

Takeaway - Krishna teaches us that focus and determination are like superpowers—they help you stay on track and achieve amazing things. He explains that people with a clear purpose have their eyes set on one target, while those who are unsure or easily distracted end up scattering their energy in a hundred directions. Arjuna was chosen for the Gita gyaan because he was curious and laser-focused. In the same way, if you, as students, want to achieve greatness, you need to stay curious and avoid distractions. It's not easy, but by training your mind to focus on what truly matters, you can overcome any temptation or challenge that comes your way.

Krishna also talks about three qualities within us: **Tamsik**, which feels fun or easy in the moment but brings trouble later (like skipping homework for video games); **Rajasik**, which keeps you busy but doesn't lead to deeper purpose (like endlessly scrolling through your phone); and **Satvik**, which might feel tough at first (like studying or exercising) but leads to long-term success and happiness. Your future depends on which of these qualities you choose to prioritize. If you spend less time on Tamsik activities, make Satvik tasks enjoyable, and find a balance to stay motivated, you'll be unstoppable.

Want to stay focused? Make distractions harder to access—like leaving your phone in another room while studying—and **reward yourself when you stick to good habits**. Think of it like this: your mind is like a garden. If you plant weeds (distractions), they'll grow wild and take over. But if you nurture it with good seeds (productive habits), you'll create something truly beautiful. So, **the choice is yours—what will you grow in your garden?**

CHAPTER SIX

The Skydiver's Leap

Avi had always loved adventure. He loved the idea of pushing himself beyond his limits, of facing challenges head-on. But there was one thing he had always been afraid of: heights.

As a child, Avi had watched in awe as his friends would climb trees, zip across rope swings, and ride roller coasters without a second thought. But not Avi. He would always stay on the ground, his heart pounding, his palms sweaty, too scared to even look at the top of the highest swings.

When Avi turned 18, his friends decided they were going to do something extreme for their last summer together before heading off to college. "We're going skydiving!" his best friend Sam announced, as he pulled out brochures for a skydiving center.

Avi froze. Skydiving? The thought of jumping out of an airplane from thousands of feet in the air made his stomach churn. "I can't do that," he said quietly. "I'm terrified of heights."

Sam and the others laughed. "Come on, Avi, it'll be amazing! You'll face your fear. You've always wanted to push yourself. This is the ultimate challenge!"

Avi hesitated. The idea of facing his fear head-on sounded thrilling, but it also terrified him. Could he really do it? Could he really jump out of an airplane and conquer his biggest fear?

Days passed, and Avi couldn't stop thinking about the skydiving trip. He kept imagining himself on the edge of the airplane, looking down at the ground below. His heart raced at the thought. But every time fear crept in, he remembered something his grandmother had told him when he was younger: *"Fear isn't something to run away from. It's a sign that you're about to do something brave."*

That thought stayed with him. Fear wasn't a reason to quit; it was a sign that he was about to challenge himself, to grow. And so, despite his nerves, Avi made a decision.

The day of the skydiving trip arrived, and Avi stood with his friends at the airstrip, watching the planes take off into the clear blue sky. His palms were clammy, his stomach twisted in knots, but he didn't back down.

As he suited up and strapped himself into the harness, his mind raced. What if he panicked mid-air? What if something went wrong?

"Are you okay, Avi?" Sam asked, noticing his worried expression.

Avi smiled nervously. "I'm scared, but I'm going to do it. I won't let fear control me."

Sam grinned. "That's the spirit! You've got this!"

Soon, Avi was climbing into the plane with his instructor, a calm, experienced skydiver named Mark. As the plane ascended, Avi's heart pounded faster. The higher they went, the more the ground below seemed to disappear. The view outside the window was breathtaking, but the thought of jumping out made his entire body tense up. He could hear his own breath, shallow and quick.

Mark noticed his unease and leaned over. "Avi, I know this is scary, but remember this: fear is just a feeling. It's not real unless you let it control you. You have the strength to push through it."

Avi nodded, though his legs felt like jelly. He had never felt so alive and so afraid at the same time.

Finally, the moment arrived. The door of the plane opened, and the rush of cold air hit Avi's face. Below him was nothing but a vast expanse of sky.

"Avi, it's time," Mark said, his voice steady. "Take a deep breath and trust yourself."

Avi closed his eyes for a brief second, remembering his grandmother's words. *Fear is a sign that you're about to do something brave.* And then, with a deep breath, Avi stepped forward. He leaped out of the plane.

For a split second, his body felt weightless, suspended in mid-air. His heart raced, his body screamed with panic, but then something incredible happened. As the wind rushed past him, he realized that fear wasn't holding him back—it was just a feeling. And that feeling was fading away with every passing second.

He spread his arms out, feeling the freedom, the exhilaration of flying. The fear that had once gripped him so tightly now seemed small, insignificant in the face of the vast, beautiful sky. He wasn't falling. He was soaring.

When the parachute deployed, the sudden jolt brought him back to the present, and Avi couldn't help but laugh. He was doing it. He was conquering his fear.

When he landed safely on the ground, his friends rushed over to him, clapping and cheering.

"Avi, that was incredible!" Sam said, his eyes wide with excitement. "You did it! You were fearless!"

Avi grinned, his heart still pounding with adrenaline. "I wasn't fearless. I was scared the whole time. But I jumped anyway. And that's what makes all the difference."He looked up at the sky, a new sense of pride filling him. Fear wasn't something to be ashamed of. Fear was simply a signal that he was about to do something amazing, something that would help him grow.

Life lesson: Be fearless.

Fear is a natural feeling, but it doesn't have to stop you. The most courageous people aren't those who never feel fear—they're the ones who face it, push through it, and do what scares them anyway.

Bhagavad Gita Shloka :
'vita-raga-bhaya-krodha man-maya mam upasritah
bahavo jnana-tapasa puta mad-bhavam agatah'
(Chapter 4, Verse 10)

Translation – 'Being freed from attachment, fear and anger, being fully absorbed in Me and taking refuge in Me, many, many persons in the past became purified by knowledge of Me - and thus they all attained transcendental love for Me.'

Takeaway - Fear and anxiety are like invisible walls that try to block your path to success. They sneak up on you when you're unsure, whisper doubts in your ear, and **make even small challenges feel like giant mountains.** The biggest troublemaker? Fear of failure. It can shake your confidence, make you second-guess yourself, and stop you from giving your best—whether it's in exams, trying new things, or simply believing in yourself.

But here's the secret: **those walls aren't real! They only exist in your mind,** and guess what? **You have the power to break through them!**

Think of fear like a shadow in a dark room—it looks huge and scary, but the moment you turn on the light of courage and confidence, it disappears! Instead of worrying about what might go wrong, focus on what you can do right now. Every time fear tries to hold you back, take a deep breath and tell yourself, "I can overcome this!"

Fear isn't a stop sign—it's an opportunity to grow stronger, braver, and more unstoppable. So go ahead, take that first step, **believe in yourself, and watch fear shrink into nothing. You are capable of more than you know!**

The Farmer and the Field of Knowledge

Mahesh was a simple farmer who lived on the edge of a quiet village. Every day, he worked tirelessly in his fields, tending to his crops and making sure the soil was rich. He woke before dawn and worked well into the evening, yet despite his hard work, something felt amiss. The harvests were never as bountiful as he hoped, and though he was physically exhausted at the end of each day, he felt a deep emptiness in his heart.

One afternoon, as Mahesh walked home after a long day in the fields, he encountered Sage Bhaskar, who was sitting beneath a large tree, meditating in silence. Mahesh paused when he saw the sage, who had a peaceful aura about him. His calmness was striking, and Mahesh couldn't help but feel drawn to him.

"Why do you look so troubled, Mahesh?" Sage Bhaskar asked without opening his eyes.

Mahesh sighed, sitting beside the sage. "I work hard on my land every day. I till the soil, plant seeds, water them, and care for them. But still, my crops don't grow as well as I would like. I feel like something is missing. What am I doing wrong?"

Sage Bhaskar opened his eyes and looked at Mahesh kindly. "The land you cultivate is like your mind. The seeds you plant in the soil are like the knowledge you choose to nurture within yourself. If you plant poor seeds or neglect them, your harvest will not be fruitful."

Mahesh frowned, not fully understanding. "But I work so hard! I put my heart into my land. What does knowledge have to do with farming?"

The sage smiled gently and patted Mahesh's shoulder. "Your mind is like a field, Mahesh. To make it fertile, you must cultivate it with wisdom, just as you cultivate the soil with care. It is through learning and understanding that the mind is nourished, and when the mind is nourished, your actions will flourish."

Mahesh thought deeply about the sage's words but remained puzzled. "But I am a simple farmer, Sage Bhaskar. I am not a scholar or a sage. How can knowledge help me grow my crops?"

Sage Bhaskar's eyes twinkled with understanding. "Knowledge doesn't just come from books, Mahesh. It's in everything around you—the way you observe nature, the way you listen, the way you reflect. Knowledge is not just facts to be memorized, but wisdom that comes from living thoughtfully. When you approach your farming with a mind that is open to learning, you will start to see things differently. You will begin to understand the language of the land itself."

Mahesh, though still unsure, felt a spark of curiosity in his heart. "So, what should I do, Sage Bhaskar?"

The sage nodded. "Start by not just working the land, but by studying it. Learn about the seasons, the soil, the plants, and the cycles of nature. And, while you are learning about your crops, open your mind to other forms of knowledge—read the teachings of great thinkers, reflect on what you learn, and allow that wisdom to guide your actions. In doing so, you will grow not only as a farmer but as a person."

For the next few weeks, Mahesh followed the sage's advice. He began to spend his evenings not only in the fields but also in the village library, where he studied farming techniques from ancient texts. He read the works of philosophers, learned about the natural world, and listened to the stories of the elders in his village. With each new piece of knowledge, Mahesh's approach to farming changed. He became more patient, more aware, and more attentive to the smallest details in his work.

He learnt when to plant, when to rest the soil, and how to listen to the wind and the birds to understand the weather patterns. He also began to look at his life more deeply, noticing how his thoughts and actions had been influenced by what he had learned.

As the seasons changed, Mahesh's harvest began to improve. His crops grew stronger, more vibrant, and more plentiful than ever before. But it wasn't just his fields that had transformed. Mahesh felt a quiet peace growing within himself, a sense of contentment that had eluded him for years. The knowledge he had gained had nourished his soul, just as it had nourished his crops.

One day, he visited Sage Bhaskar to share his gratitude. "Sage Bhaskar, I finally understand. Knowledge has not only helped me in my work, but it has also brought peace to my heart. My fields are abundant now, and my mind is at ease."

Sage Bhaskar smiled, his eyes filled with wisdom. "That is the beauty of knowledge, Mahesh. It is like the rain that falls on a thirsty land, or the sunlight that nurtures a growing plant. When you open your mind to learning, you are planting seeds that will one day grow into wisdom and peace."

Mahesh bowed respectfully. "Thank you, Sage Bhaskar. I will continue to tend to both my fields and my mind with the same care and devotion."And from that day forward, Mahesh not only worked the land with greater skill but also cultivated a mind full of wisdom, and his heart remained at peace.

Life lesson: Seek knowledge.

Just as a field requires knowledge and care to yield a bountiful harvest, our minds need wisdom to cultivate peace and understanding. The more we nurture our minds with learning and reflection, the more abundant our lives will become. Knowledge is the key to purifying our thoughts and bringing us closer to inner peace.

Bhagavad Gita Shloka :
*'na hi jnanena sadrsam pavitram iha vidyate
tat svayam yoga-samsiddhah kalenatmani vindati'*
(Chapter 4, Verse 38)

Translation – 'In this world there is nothing so sublime and pure as transcendental knowledge. Such knowledge is the mature fruit of all mysticism. One who has become accomplished in the practice of devotional service enjoys this knowledge within himself in due course of time.'

Takeaway - Krishna teaches us that **knowledge is like a bright light—it clears away confusion, fear, and negative thoughts.** But here's the thing: it's not just about memorizing facts for exams! **Real knowledge is about understanding life, making wise choices, and growing into the best version of yourself.** When you truly learn with an open heart, you gain clarity, confidence, and inner peace—like switching on a light in a dark room!

But this magic only happens when you're curious, humble, and eager to learn. That's why it's so important to respect your teachers, seek wisdom with an open mind, and never stop exploring new ideas.

Knowledge isn't just about getting good grades—it's about connecting your heart and mind to something greater. When you learn with sincerity and purpose, life makes more sense, and you start seeing challenges as opportunities instead of roadblocks. **It helps you trust that everything happens for a reason** and that you're on the right path, even when things seem uncertain.

The best part? **True knowledge doesn't just fill your brain—it fills your life with joy, purpose, and strength. It helps you make** better decisions, build meaningful relationships, and stay calm even when life throws challenges your way. When you learn with love and devotion, you start seeing the world in a whole new way—one filled with endless possibilities.

So keep learning, keep growing, and keep turning on the light! Because **the brighter your knowledge, the brighter your future.**

CHAPTER EIGHT

Arjuna's Dilemma

Once upon a time, in the midst of the great battlefield of Kurukshetra, Arjuna, the mighty warrior, stood frozen in fear and doubt. His hands trembled as he held the Gandiva, his powerful bow, but he could not bring himself to pull the string. Before him stood the Kaurava army—his cousins, uncles, and even his beloved teacher, Dronacharya. The weight of the battle, the thought of fighting his own family, felt like a heavy burden on his heart.

"Arjuna, why do you hesitate?" Lord Krishna, his charioteer and mentor, asked with a voice calm yet filled with wisdom.

Arjuna's voice quivered with uncertainty. "How can I fight, Krishna? If I fight, I will kill those who have loved me, those who have taught me. But if I don't fight, I will betray my duty as a warrior. Both choices seem unbearable."

Krishna looked at him with compassion, his voice filled with clarity. "Arjuna, you stand at a crossroads. Life is full of choices. You may not always be able to see the full picture, but every choice you make shapes your future. What you choose today will define who you become tomorrow."

"But Krishna," Arjuna replied, "How can I make the right choice when both paths seem filled with sorrow and loss?"

Krishna, noticing the struggle in Arjuna's heart, spoke with deep understanding. "Let me explain it to you through a simple lesson. Imagine a gardener planting a tree. He chooses to plant the seed, water it, and nurture it every day. Slowly, with time, the tree grows strong, and in its fullness, it provides shade and fruit for others. Had the gardener not made the choice to plant that seed, the tree would never have existed."

Arjuna, listening intently, asked, "But Krishna, how does this apply to my dilemma? My choices will hurt those I love."

Krishna smiled gently. "Arjuna, just like the gardener chooses to plant a seed, the choices you make today plant the seeds of your future. It's not only the action but the intention behind the action that matters. You are at a turning point, and this moment, this decision, will define who you are. You must choose the path that aligns with your dharma—your higher purpose."

Arjuna looked at the battlefield, feeling torn. Krishna continued, "There are two paths before you. One is the path of comfort, where you seek to avoid the hard truths, where you follow the voice of fear and desire. This path leads to regret and stagnation. The other path is the path of righteousness. It requires sacrifice, effort, and courage. It is not easy, but it leads to lasting fulfillment and growth."

Arjuna struggled with the weight of his choice, but Krishna offered one more analogy: "Imagine you are an archer. You stand before a target. There are distractions all around you—the noise of the world, the wind, your doubts. You can either focus on these distractions or choose to focus on the target. The archer who is distracted will never hit the mark. But the one who chooses to focus, who stays steady in his aim, will always succeed."

Arjuna's mind began to clear. He realized that his confusion and fear had been distractions, pulling him away from his true purpose. This battle was not just a war between two armies, but a test of his resolve, his values, and his ability to act in alignment with his dharma, his greater purpose.With renewed determination, Arjuna grasped his Gandiva with strength and clarity. He looked at Krishna and declared, "I understand now. Life is a result of the choices we make. I choose the path of righteousness, no matter how difficult the road ahead may be."

Life lesson: Your life is a result of your choices.

Our life is a result of the choices we make. Each decision we face, no matter how small, shapes our destiny. The easy path may seem inviting, but it often leads to regret. The righteous path requires courage, sacrifice, and discipline, but it leads to growth, fulfillment, and lasting happiness.

Act with intention and awareness. Life is not about escaping difficult choices; it is about making the right ones, aligned with our values and higher purpose. The choices we make today plant the seeds for the life we will live.

Bhagavad Gita Shloka :
'iti te jnanam akhyatam guhyad guhyataram maya
vimrsyaitad asesena yathecchasi tatha kuru'
(Chapter 18, Verse 63)

Translation – 'Thus I have explained to you knowledge still more confidential. Deliberate on this fully and then do what you wish to do.'

Takeaway - Krishna teaches us that **our lives are built on the choices we make**—like a giant puzzle where every decision adds a new piece. Some choices help us move forward, while others hold us back. The cool part? **You're the one in control!**

Every small decision—whether to study or scroll on your phone, help a friend or ignore them, give up or keep trying—shapes your future. The Bhagavad Gita reminds us that we always have the power to choose. Even when things get tough, you can decide to face challenges head-on, learn from mistakes, and grow stronger.

Think of life like a video game —every choice unlocks a new level. If you keep avoiding the hard stuff, making excuses, or waiting for luck to fix things, you'll stay stuck. But if you focus, work hard, and take smart actions, you'll unlock new opportunities, success, and a life you're proud of.

The best part? You don't need to be perfect—just be mindful of your choices. **Every good decision you make today is a step toward a happier, more successful, and more exciting future. So, what will you choose? To sit back or to level up?**

CHAPTER NINE

The Envious Crow

In a peaceful forest, a crow lived a simple, content life. Its dark, sleek feathers blended with the shadows of the trees, and it was happy with the rhythm of its days—perching on branches, hopping along the forest floor, and flying through the cool, open skies. Yet, despite this happiness, the crow couldn't shake the feeling that there was something missing.

One day, while flying over a serene lake, the crow saw a swan gliding gracefully across the water. Its feathers were a brilliant white, glowing like snow under the sunlight. The crow couldn't help but stare in awe at the swan's beauty. "That must be the happiest bird in the world," the crow thought. "Look at how pure and beautiful it is compared to my dull black feathers."

Curious and envious, the crow flew over to the swan. "Excuse me, beautiful swan," the crow said, "You must be the happiest bird in the world with your dazzling white feathers."

The swan looked at the crow, its eyes thoughtful. "I thought I was happy," the swan replied, "But then I saw a parrot. The parrot has two bright, beautiful colors—green and red—while I am just plain white. So, I thought the parrot must be the happiest bird."

The crow's curiosity only grew. "The parrot must be the happiest bird, then!" it thought. So, it flew off to find the parrot. Upon reaching a tall tree, the crow perched next to the parrot. "You must be the happiest bird in the world with your lovely green and red feathers," the crow said.

The parrot blinked and shook its head. "I thought I was happy," the parrot replied, "But then I saw a peacock. The peacock has so many vibrant colors! It is admired by everyone. I wish I could have all those colors, too."

The crow, now more curious than ever, flew to find the peacock. It traveled far and wide, until it came to a zoo where a magnificent peacock strutted proudly. The crow saw people gathered around, taking pictures and admiring the bird's beautiful feathers, sparkling like jewels in the sunlight. Envious of the attention the peacock received, the crow called out, "You must be the happiest bird in the world, with so many colors and admirers."

The peacock let out a deep sigh, its tail feathers fluttering slightly. "I was happy," it said, "Until I was captured and placed here in this zoo. I no longer have the freedom to roam the earth, to fly where I wish. You, crow, have something far more precious than my feathers or my admirers—you have your freedom."

The crow sat silently for a moment, the words of the peacock echoing in its mind. It had been so consumed by what it didn't have—so focused on the dazzling feathers of the swan, the vibrant colors of the parrot, and the admiration that surrounded the peacock—that it had failed to see the treasure that had been with it all along: its freedom.

The crow stretched its wings and soared high into the sky, feeling the wind beneath it, lifting it higher and higher. As it flew, it marveled at the vastness of the world—the sprawling forests, the sparkling lakes, and the endless blue of the sky. It could go anywhere, do anything, and see the world from countless perspectives. The crow realized how much it had taken this freedom for granted. While the swan, the parrot, and the peacock were all confined to their own worlds, each of them had something that the crow didn't: limitations.

The crow's wings beat strongly as it flew in wide circles above the forest, and for the first time, it felt truly alive. The beauty of the world around it became clearer than ever before. It could fly freely, explore new places, and experience the world without being tied to any one spot. The crow laughed to itself, feeling a sense of joy it had never known before. "What more could I want?" it thought. "I already have everything I need."

The crow continued flying until the sun began to dip low on the horizon. It then made its way back to the familiar, peaceful forest where it had always felt at home. As the crow perched on its favorite branch, it looked out over the landscape below, watching the world slowly fade into twilight. The stars began to twinkle in the sky, and the cool breeze gently rustled the leaves.

The crow sat there, heart full, a smile spreading across its beak. "I have my own blessings," it thought again, "and they are enough." The simple, everyday joys—the feeling of the wind against its feathers, the freedom to fly, the beauty of the world around it—were all it needed to feel complete. The crow had always been enough just as it was, and that realization filled it with peace.

"I don't need to be like anyone else," the crow whispered to the night. "I am happy just being me." With that, the crow closed its eyes, feeling a deep sense of gratitude wash over it. The comparisons, the envy, and the longing for what others had were all gone, replaced by a quiet contentment. The crow had found its place in the world—one where it could simply be itself, free and happy.And so, from that day forward, the crow no longer looked to others for validation or sought what it didn't have. It embraced its own life, its own blessings, and found joy in the freedom to be exactly who it was, no comparisons necessary.

Life lesson: Avoid jealousy & comparisons.

Jealousy often arises when we compare our lives to others. But the truth is, everyone has their own unique blessings and challenges. Instead of chasing what others have, we should focus on the gifts and blessings in our own lives. True happiness comes from within, from appreciating what we already have.

Bhagavad Gita Shloka :
*'advesta sarva-bhutanam maitrah karuna eva ca
nirmamo nirahankarah sama-duhkha-sukhah ksami'*
(Chapter 12, Verse 13)

Translation – 'One who is not envious but is a kind friend to all living entities, who does not think himself a proprietor and is free from false ego, who is equal in both happiness and distress, who is tolerant – such a devotee is dear to Me.'

Takeaway - Jealousy sneaks in when we compare ourselves to others—whether it's grades, talents, or achievements. It makes us feel like someone else's success takes away from our own. But here's the truth: It doesn't!

Krishna teaches that **we are all connected—each of us has our own unique journey. Instead of feeling jealous, celebrate others' wins and focus on improving yourself.** Imagine if, instead of feeling bad when a friend succeeds, you felt genuinely happy for them—how amazing would that be? Their talents don't limit yours; they inspire you to reach your own full potential.

Feeling insecure when someone is excelling at something you love? **Instead of envy, see it as proof of what's possible! If they can do it, so can you—in your own way, at your own pace.** The universe, or a higher power, isn't playing favorites. Your time will come if you stay focused on your growth instead of distractions.

The divine isn't just found in temples, prayers, or rituals—it's everywhere, woven into the world around us. It's in the brilliant colors of an artist's painting, the soothing melody of a musician's song, the graceful movements of a dancer, and the unstoppable determination of an athlete. Every skill, every talent, every beautiful moment is a reflection of something greater—a spark of divinity expressing itself in different ways.When you stop seeing others as competition and start seeing them as inspiration, you free yourself from jealousy and open the door to success, happiness, and real confidence. **So, next time you see someone succeed, don't let jealousy hold you back—let inspiration lift you up! Cheer for others, believe in yourself, and watch how amazing life becomes!**

CHAPTER TEN

The Mountain and the Clouds

Anuja lived in a small village nestled between rolling hills, where the air was always fresh, and the sunsets painted the skies in beautiful hues of red and orange. From a young age, she was taught that happiness was something you could get—something you could own. More clothes, more food, more possessions. The more she had, the more she believed she would feel satisfied. But no matter how much she acquired, there was always a sense of emptiness inside her, as if something was missing. Each new desire she fulfilled left her with another, and the cycle continued. It felt as though no matter how much she had, it was never enough.

One afternoon, as she walked along a familiar path near the village, her mind filled with restless thoughts, Anuja noticed an old woman sitting by the side of the road. Her name was Maya, and she was known throughout the village for her calm and wise demeanor. She was often seen sitting quietly, content in her own company, with a peaceful smile on her face.

Seeing Anuja lost in thought, Maya called out to her. "You seem troubled, my dear. What's on your mind?"

Anuja sighed and sat down beside Maya, feeling a sense of comfort in her presence. "I've been feeling so restless," she confessed. "No matter what I get, no matter how much I have, it's never enough. I keep chasing after things—new clothes, more money, a bigger house—and yet, there's always this emptiness inside of me."

Maya nodded gently, her eyes filled with understanding. "I see," she said softly, and then her gaze turned to the mountain in the distance, its peak standing tall against the sky, unchanged by the passing of time. "Look at that mountain, Anuja. No matter how many clouds drift by, the mountain remains unmoved, solid, and grounded."

Anuja followed her gaze, but she was still unsure. "But the clouds move constantly, don't they? The mountain stands still while the clouds pass by. What does that have to do with me?"

Maya smiled kindly, her voice steady. "The clouds are like desires, Anuja. They come and go, constantly shifting and changing. You might chase after one, thinking it will bring you happiness, but once it's gone, another desire appears, and the cycle starts again. But the mountain doesn't chase the clouds, nor does it get disturbed by them. It simply remains there, unmoved. It doesn't depend on the clouds to define its existence."

Anuja furrowed her brow, trying to understand. "But how can I be like that mountain? I'm always running after the clouds. If I stop, I'm afraid I'll miss out on something."

Maya chuckled softly, her eyes twinkling with warmth. "It's not about running away from your desires, Anuja. It's about learning not to let them control you. Desires will always come, just like the clouds will always pass. The key is not to let them dictate how you feel. Like the mountain, you must remain grounded in your true nature, knowing that happiness doesn't come from chasing after every fleeting wish. True peace comes from accepting what you already have and being present in the moment."

Anuja's heart stirred with something deep inside her. For the first time, she realized that the emptiness she felt wasn't because she didn't have enough—it was because she hadn't stopped to appreciate what she already had. She had a loving family, a beautiful village, friends who cared about her, and a heart full of dreams. She had always thought happiness was something to be gained, but now she understood it was something to be found within, in the present moment.

Maya continued, "When you stop chasing the clouds, you'll make room for the sunshine to fill your life. The mountain doesn't chase after the clouds—it stands still, and in doing so, it allows everything around it to fall into place. You, too, can find peace when you stop rushing and simply be still."

Anuja's eyes brightened with understanding. "I think I get it now, Maya. Happiness doesn't come from getting everything I want. It comes from being content with what I have."

Maya nodded, her smile widening. "Exactly, Anuja. True peace comes not from chasing after things, but from realizing that what you already have is enough. Be still, be grounded, and you will find the happiness that has been there all along."

From that day forward, Anuja worked on shifting her mindset. She stopped chasing every passing desire, and instead, she focused on the simple joys of her life. She still had goals, dreams, and things she wished to accomplish, but they no longer controlled her thoughts or actions. She learned to appreciate the quiet moments—the sound of birds singing at dawn, the warm hug of her mother when she came home, the laughter shared with friends over a cup of tea. Each small moment felt rich and meaningful in a way it never had before.

Anuja also began to notice how her relationships with others changed. She wasn't constantly trying to impress anyone or keep up with the latest trends. She simply enjoyed being herself, knowing that she didn't need to compare herself to anyone else to feel good. She could enjoy the beauty of the world around her without feeling like she was missing out.

Slowly, Anuja found a sense of peace she had never known. The restlessness faded, and in its place was a quiet contentment, like the mountain standing strong in the midst of changing clouds. She realized that happiness wasn't tied to what she had or how much she could acquire. It was in how she responded to life, how she embraced the present, and how she viewed the world through the lens of gratitude and self-acceptance. Her desires no longer controlled her. She learned to focus on what truly mattered—family, love, and the present moment. The more she stood firm, like the mountain, the more she realized that peace was always within her reach. Quiet, steady, and enduring.

Life lesson: Control your desires.

True peace doesn't come from fulfilling every desire, but from understanding that happiness is found within. When we stop chasing after fleeting things and focus on what really matters, we become like the mountain—grounded, strong, and at peace with ourselves.

Bhagavad Gita Shloka :
'dhyayato visayan pumsah sangas tesupajayate
sangat sanjayate kamah kamat krodho bhijayate'
(Chapter 2 , Verse 62)

Translation – 'While contemplating the objects of the senses, a person develops attachment for them and from such attachment lust develops and from lust anger arises.'

Takeaway - Ever wanted something so badly that you couldn't stop thinking about it? Maybe it's a new phone, more followers, or winning a competition. Krishna explains that **when we get attached to something, it turns into desire, and when we don't get it, frustration and anger take over.** And guess what? This cycle never ends! **The more we get, the more we want—it's like a never-ending hunger for "more."**

Think of it like scrolling through social media. You see someone with the latest sneakers or a cool new gadget, and suddenly, you feel like you need it too! But stop and ask yourself: Will this really make me happy? Or is it just a passing craving? Most of the time, these desires trick us into thinking we can't be happy without them. But the truth is, **happiness isn't in things—it's in how we think!**

So, how do you break free? **Catch your desires early—before they take over your mind.** When you start craving something, pause and ask yourself: "Do I really need this, or is it just FOMO?" Instead of letting temporary wants control you, redirect your energy! Use your desire for success to push yourself to work harder, your desire for attention to build real connections, and your desire for happiness to help others.

Desires will always exist—but you get to decide which ones are worth chasing!When you learn to control your mind instead of letting it control you, you unlock true freedom and peace, no matter what the world throws at you.

CHAPTER ELEVEN

Zen Kavi

Once upon a time, in a small village surrounded by rolling hills and quiet forests, there lived a curious and lively boy named Kavi. Kavi had a big heart, but he often struggled with his emotions. When something went wrong, he would get upset or frustrated, and when things went well, he couldn't help but get overly excited. His emotions were like a rollercoaster, making him feel like he had no control over how he reacted.

One warm afternoon, as Kavi was walking through the village, he spotted Anish, the wisest man in the village, sitting quietly under a tree. Anish was always calm, no matter what happened around him. The villagers often spoke about how he seemed to stay steady and peaceful, no matter the circumstances. Curious, Kavi approached him.

"Anish, I've noticed you're always calm, no matter what happens. How do you do it?" Kavi asked, looking up at him with wide eyes.

Anish smiled and invited Kavi to sit beside him. "Would you like to hear a story that might help you understand?" he asked.

Kavi nodded eagerly, and Anish began.

"Long ago, in a village much like ours, there lived a wise teacher named Sita. One year, the village went through a terrible drought. The crops dried up, the rivers shrank, and the villagers became anxious and fearful. Yet, Sita remained calm. When people came to her for advice, they asked, 'Sita, how can you stay so peaceful when everything is falling apart around us?'"

"Sita replied, 'The drought is part of the world's cycle. Things change, and we can't control that. But how we see the situation—our perspective—can make all the difference. When we choose to see things with a calm mind, we can handle any storm.'"

"The villagers were amazed, but they still struggled to understand. Then, after a few months, the rains finally came. The crops grew back, and the village rejoiced. But Sita, instead of getting caught up in the excitement like everyone else, simply smiled and said, 'Happiness is like the rain—it comes and goes. But our peace? That's something we can choose, no matter what.'"

Kavi listened closely, absorbing every word.

"So, Anish," Kavi said thoughtfully, "are you saying that it's not what happens around us that matters, but how we choose to see it?"

Anish nodded. "Exactly, Kavi. Our perspective shapes how we feel. If we focus only on the good or the bad, we'll always be tossed around by life's ups and downs. But if we learn to see everything through the lens of understanding—knowing that good and bad are just part of life—we can stay steady, no matter what."

Kavi thought about this deeply. The next day, as the village prepared for a big festival, Kavi could hardly contain his excitement. There were games, music, and delicious food. He rushed to join his friends, but then he remembered what Anish had said. Instead of running ahead, Kavi took a deep breath, grounded himself, and said, "I'll enjoy this moment, but I won't let it control me."

Later that day, while playing a game, Kavi accidentally lost his favorite toy in the crowd. At first, he felt a wave of frustration, but then he paused. He remembered Anish's words about perspective. "It's just a toy," Kavi thought. "I can choose how I see this. It's not the end of the world. Maybe I'll find something even more fun to do."

Instead of feeling upset, Kavi chose to see the situation calmly. He found new friends to play with and had a great time without his toy.

From that day on, Kavi began to practice the power of perspective. He realized that when he shifted how he saw things, he could remain peaceful, no matter the circumstances. Whether it was a happy moment or a difficult one, Kavi knew that peace came from within, not from what happened around him.From that day on, whenever someone asked Kavi how he managed to stay so calm, he would smile and say, 'True peace isn't about what happens around us, it's about how we handle what's inside. When you learn to stay calm in the storm, you find the peace that's always been there.' And with that simple wisdom, Kavi helped others discover the calm within themselves too.

Life lesson: Develop the right perspective.

The way we choose to see things shapes how we feel. By developing the right perspective, we can find peace, no matter what life brings our way.

Bhagavad Gita Shloka :
'duhkhesv anudvigna-manah sukhesu vigata-sprhah
vita-raga-bhaya-krodhah sthita-dhir munir ucyate'
(Chapter 2, Verse 56)

Translation – 'One who is not disturbed in mind even amidst the threefold miseries or elated when there is happiness and who is free from attachment, fear and anger is called a sage of steady mind.'

Takeaway - Life can feel like a rollercoaster—one moment, everything's great, and the next, things aren't going your way. But Krishna teaches us a superpower—staying calm no matter what happens! **A wise person doesn't get too excited when things go well or too upset when things go wrong.They stay balanced—free from fear, anger, and over-attachment.** Why? Because they see things as they really are instead of letting emotions take over.

Imagine you're in a tough exam. You can either panic and freeze or stay calm, think clearly, and do your best. Which one sounds better? Exactly! **When you learn to keep your cool, you make smarter decisions, handle challenges better, and feel less stressed.**

Instead of worrying about what might happen, focus on what you can control. The Bhagavad Gita reminds us that tough times don't last forever—just like storms pass, so do problems. When you stop fighting against life and go with the flow, you'll find clarity, confidence, and peace.

Want to master this? **Train your mind like a warrior!** Control your thoughts, focus on the present, and remember **a calm mind is the strongest mind.** The more you practice, the easier life becomes. So, are you ready to take charge?

The more you practice, the easier life becomes. So, **are you ready to take charge?**

Abhilasha's Battle with the Clock

Abhilasha sat at her desk, the hands of the clock ticking away, each second louder than the last. The final exams were only a few days away, and yet her textbooks remained closed. Her mind was a whirlwind of thoughts—thoughts of everything she could do except study. Her phone buzzed with a message from her best friend, Riya.

"Hey, how's the studying going?" Riya's text popped up on the screen.

Abhilasha sighed and glanced at the clock again. "Not good. I just can't get myself to focus."

"You should start now," Riya replied. "It's all about discipline. If you control your time, you'll feel so much more at ease."

Abhilasha tossed her phone onto the bed, rolling her eyes. "I've heard that a million times before. But, it's always so much easier to put things off," she muttered to herself. "Maybe I'll start after a quick nap. Or... maybe I'll just watch one episode of that show I've been dying to catch up on."

As she picked up the remote, a wave of guilt swept over her. She had always been the last-minute type, hoping that cramming everything into one intense night of studying would somehow be enough. But this time, she had a sinking feeling that her usual strategy might not work.

The next day, in class, Abhilasha struggled to concentrate. Her mind wandered, drifting from the lesson to the upcoming exams, then to thoughts of her unfinished assignments. Her teacher, Mr. Sharma, noticed her distraction.

"Is something troubling you, Abhilasha?" he asked, his voice soft yet concerned.

Abhilasha hesitated, then sighed. "I just can't seem to focus, sir. I always put things off until the last minute, and now it feels like it's too late. I've wasted so much time."

Mr. Sharma smiled kindly, putting down his pen. "Abhilasha, discipline isn't about waiting until you feel motivated. It's about making a plan and sticking to it, even when it feels hard. The more disciplined you become, the easier things will start to feel. You don't need to be perfect; you just need to show up and do the work, one step at a time."

Abhilasha looked down at her desk, feeling a spark of hope. Could it really be that simple? She had always heard that self-discipline was key, but hearing it from her teacher made her realize that she could actually take control, starting right now.

That evening, Abhilasha decided to try something different. She sat down at her desk and opened her study materials. Instead of aiming to study for hours straight, she set a simple rule for herself: one hour of studying, followed by a 15-minute break. No distractions. No checking her phone. Just studying.

At first, it felt unnatural. Her mind kept wandering to everything else—her friends, what she'd wear for the weekend, the book she wanted to finish reading. But she stuck with it. Slowly, the time started to pass more quickly. By the end of the hour, she realized that the world hadn't ended, and in fact, she had actually learned something. She felt a strange sense of accomplishment.

The next day, she stuck to the same plan. One hour of study, then a break. Then another hour. She began to feel less overwhelmed as she covered more material, and the weight of her stress started to lift. The pressure didn't feel so suffocating anymore.

As the days passed, Abhilasha continued to follow her new study routine. Each hour of work brought her closer to the goal, but it also brought her something else: peace. The quiet, focused rhythm of studying wasn't just productive; it felt grounding. She began to realize that discipline wasn't about pushing herself when she felt like it—it was about showing up consistently, even when it was tough. And the more she practiced this, the easier it became.

The night before the exams, Abhilasha sat in her room, reviewing her notes. She didn't feel frantic or anxious. She felt ready. The hours of work she had put in, step by step, had prepared her not only for the exams but for life beyond them. She had learned that self-discipline wasn't about being perfect—it was about the simple act of taking small steps every day, even when it felt hard.

The next day, as she walked into the exam hall, Abhilasha felt a calmness that surprised her. She wasn't stressing about whether she had studied enough; she had done the work, and now it was time to show what she knew.

When the results came, Abhilasha had done well. More importantly, she had discovered the power of self-discipline and the sense of peace that came with it. She realized that the more she controlled her time and focused on what mattered, the more her life fell into balance. It was no longer about waiting for motivation to strike; it was about creating a routine that worked, and sticking to it—even when she didn't feel like it.

Life lesson: Follow discipline in life.

Self-discipline is the key to achieving your goals with a peaceful mind. It's not about waiting for the perfect moment; it's about showing up every day, doing the work, and taking control of your time. With discipline, challenges become easier to face, and the path to success becomes clearer.

Bhagavad Gita Shloka :
'yuktahara-viharasya yukta-cestasya karmasu
yukta-svapnavabodhasya yogo bhavati duhkha-ha'
(Chapter 6 , Verse 17)

Translation – 'He who is regulated in his habits of eating, sleeping, recreation and work can mitigate all material pains by practicing the yoga system.'

Takeaway - Ever wondered why some people seem to achieve their dreams while others keep struggling? **The secret isn't luck—it's discipline!Krishna teaches us that balance is the key to success—**whether it's eating, working, or resting. A life that's too extreme in any direction can lead to burnout or laziness. But when you master self-discipline, you can stay focused, make steady progress, and still have time for fun!

Think of discipline like leveling up in a video game . You don't beat the game in one go—you win by practicing, improving, and staying consistent. The same goes for real life! Want to ace your exams, become a great athlete, or master a skill? Set goals, create a schedule, and stay committed! Even small, daily habits—like waking up on time, limiting distractions, and staying organized—help train your mind to stay on track.

Need some **pro tips to boost your discipline? Start by breaking big tasks into smaller steps** so they feel more manageable, and **create a study schedule** that you actually stick to. **Limit distractions**—yes, that means putting your phone away or keeping it in another room while studying! **Take short breaks** to refresh your mind, but don't let them turn into long distractions. **Getting enough sleep** is also crucial because your brain needs time to recharge and stay sharp. **Most importantly, stay patient and positive with yourself—discipline isn't about being perfect, it's about being consistent.** The more you practice, the stronger your self-control becomes, and soon, staying focused and productive will feel natural! **A disciplined mind is unstoppable! So, are you ready to take charge and make your dreams happen?**

The Reluctant Scholar

As Aarav sat at his desk, the ticking of the clock seemed to echo louder in his ears with each passing second. His board exams were just a week away, and the pressure weighed heavily on him. The books in front of him were like towering mountains—each page felt like a steep incline, one he had to climb but didn't want to. The hours of studying were endless, and with each page he turned, the bright world of games, laughter, and freedom outside seemed to pull him further away.

The afternoon sun streamed through the window, casting a warm glow across the room, but Aarav barely noticed. His mind wandered to the games room downstairs, where his friends were gathered, laughing and playing their favorite games. The sound of their excitement made his frustration even worse. How he longed to be with them, to take a break from the monotony of studying and simply relax.

He glanced at his textbooks—subjects he had already studied a thousand times, but they still felt as foreign as the first day. "What's the point?" he thought, staring at the page in front of him. "All this studying... it's never-ending! Why am I torturing myself with this? Life could be so much more fun if I could just spend my time playing with my friends. This exam is just a meaningless task. It feels like I'm wasting my time—time I could be living, experiencing, and enjoying."

Aarav slammed his book shut in frustration and leaned back in his chair. He stared out the window, watching his friends, who were completely carefree, laughing and enjoying life. He could hear their laughter drifting through the window. For a moment, he just sat there, wondering why he was putting himself through the grind while they were making the most of their time. "Why am I doing this?" he thought again. "Is this really worth it?"

He let out a deep sigh, feeling trapped by the weight of his books and his own thoughts. It felt like the rest of his life was on pause while his friends were out living in full color.

His mother, hearing the soft sighs of her son, walked into his room with a gentle smile. She noticed how he had slouched in his chair, the books scattered across the desk. "Aarav," she said calmly, "I see you're having a hard time focusing today. What's on your mind?"

Aarav slumped further in his chair. "Mom, it's not fair! All my friends are out having fun, and I'm stuck here with all these books. I don't feel like studying anymore. Why can't I just take a break like everyone else? It feels like I'm missing out on life."

His mother sat beside him, her expression soft but firm. She placed a hand on his shoulder and looked him in the eye. "I understand, Aarav. It's tough. But remember, life isn't just about the immediate pleasures; it's about fulfilling your duties first. And right now, your duty is to study hard and do your best in your exams. That's the responsibility you've taken on as a student."

Aarav looked up, slightly confused. "What Mom, I don't feel like studying at all?"

She smiled gently. "Well, you see, your responsibility right now is to study. You don't just study for the sake of grades or marks. You study so that you can create a better future for yourself—and your family. By doing well, you will become the ray of hope for those who are counting on you. You have to put in the effort now, so that later, you can live the life you dreamt of."

Aarav was still uncertain. "But what he moments of enjoyment I am missing out on, Mom? Everyone else is out there enjoying life, and I'm here stuck with these books."

His mother nodded, understanding his frustration. "I know it's hard, my dear. But think about it this way: what if you could be the one who inspires others? What if your hard work today could light up the future of not just your own life, but the lives of your family and even your community?"

Aarav thought about this for a moment, but his mind still wandered to his friends outside. Sensing his unease, his mother decided to tell him a story.

"Do you remember Dr. Ramesh, the doctor who helps so many people in our town?" she asked. Aarav nodded. He had seen Dr. Ramesh many times—always busy, always focused on his patients, and always in high demand.

"When Dr. Ramesh was your age, he was just like you—studying late into the night while his friends were out playing. He didn't have the luxury of taking breaks or chasing immediate pleasures. His duty, just like yours now, was to focus on his studies. He worked tirelessly, day in and day out, never complaining. While others were relaxing, he was mastering his subjects. He understood that the success he wanted could only be achieved through consistent effort."

Aarav's eyes widened as he listened closely.

"Dr. Ramesh has now become a renowned doctor. He not only provides medical care to the people in our neighbourhood, but he also conducts free health camps for the underprivileged. Today, he's not just earning a good living—he's making a real difference in society, saving lives and changing people's futures. And do you know the most amazing part? He's a beacon of hope for those who need him, and he's admired by everyone. People look up to him not just for his success, but for the sacrifices he made during his student life. They look at him and say, 'If he can do it, so can I!'

Aarav sat quietly, absorbing the weight of his mother's words. She smiled gently. "Aarav, you see, your responsibility is bigger than just studying to pass exams. Your hard work now will shape your future and your ability to contribute to society. The sacrifices you make today—just like Dr. Ramesh—will one day allow you to inspire others. Imagine if, one day, someone looks at you and says, 'If Aarav could do it, I can do it too.' Your actions today can become the light for others to follow."

Aarav sat still, his thoughts racing. He could feel the heaviness of responsibility, but also the spark of purpose. He realized that the short-term pleasures were fleeting, but the long-term rewards of hard work and responsibility would last a lifetime. He wanted to be the one who inspired others to believe in themselves, and to take responsibility for their own futures. But he knew, deep down, that this would not come through shortcuts or avoiding his responsibilities. If he was to become that person—someone whose life was a model of hard work and achievement—he had to embrace the present, no matter how difficult it felt.

"Alright, Mom," Aarav said, determination slowly building within him. "I understand now. I'll focus on my studies. I'll do my best, not just for myself, but for everyone who believes in me."

His mother gave him a warm smile, proud of her son. "That's the spirit, Aarav. When you fulfill your duties, you not only build a better life for yourself, but you also become a source of inspiration for others."

A determined Aarav stood up from his desk and walked over to his dartboard hanging on the wall. For a brief moment, he needed a break—a chance to clear his mind and refocus. He picked up a dart, aimed carefully, and threw it. The dart flew across the room and landed just a little off-center. Aarav frowned, but without hesitation, he pulled another dart from the tray. This time, he adjusted his stance and focused intently, his eyes locking on the bullseye. He threw again. The dart landed closer to the center, but not quite there yet. Aarav took a deep breath, letting the frustration roll off him, and picked up the third dart. His hands were steady now, his focus sharp. He knew he couldn't force it, but with patience, he could get it right.

This time, when he threw the dart, it hit the bullseye perfectly. Aarav grinned in satisfaction, a sense of accomplishment filling him. It wasn't just about the game—it was about the lesson he was learning in that moment. He had to practice, focus, and keep pushing forward. Just like with the darts, life would sometimes feel off-center, and things wouldn't always go as planned. But if he stayed determined, if he kept aiming for his goals, eventually, he'd hit the mark.

With a deep breath, Aarav turned away from the dartboard and walked back to his desk. A calm, steady energy flowed through him now. The doubts and distractions had melted away, replaced by a newfound sense of purpose. He sat down, picked up his pen, and began studying again. His mind was clearer, his focus stronger. He knew that every moment he spent working toward his goal—no matter how small—was bringing him closer to the person he wanted to be.Just like Dr. Ramesh, the doctor his mother had spoken of, Aarav wanted to be someone who inspired others through dedication and hard work. He wanted to be someone whose efforts would make a difference in the world. It wasn't about immediate rewards; it was about becoming the kind of person who could change lives with the work they put in. And with that thought in mind, Aarav immersed himself in his studies with renewed vigor, fully aware that the road to success wasn't always easy, but it was always worth it.

Life lesson: Fulfill your duties.

One should act according to their duty and responsibilities, without hesitation or doubt. Sometimes, fulfilling our duty requires hard choices, but it is important to stay focused on what is right and not to shy away from responsibilities, especially when they are aligned with justice and dharma.

Bhagavad Gita Shloka :
'sva dharmam api caveksya na vikampitum arhasi
dharmyad dhi yuddhac chreyo 'nyat ksatriyasya na vidyate'
(Chapter 2, Verse 31)

Translation – 'Considering your specific duty as a ksatriya, you should know that there is no better engagement for you than fighting on religious principles and so there is no need for hesitation.'

Takeaway - Imagine standing in the middle of a battlefield, unsure of what to do next. That's exactly how Arjuna felt—torn between his emotions and his duty. He didn't want to fight because he was afraid of hurting his loved ones. But Krishna reminded him that **as a Kshatriya (warrior), his duty was to fight for justice,** even when it felt difficult. His purpose was bigger than his fears.

Now, you might not be in an actual battle, but you do have challenges to face—like school, exams, responsibilities, and tough decisions. **As a student, your battlefield is your classroom, and your duty is to learn and grow!** Sometimes studying feels hard, boring, or even impossible, but Krishna teaches us that true strength comes from staying committed, even when things get tough.

Doubt and hesitation only make us weaker, but determination turns us into warriors! Instead of running away from challenges, face them head-on with confidence. Every time you push through a tough lesson, stay focused on your studies, or refuse to give up, you are proving to yourself that you are stronger than your fears.

A warrior doesn't quit in the middle of battle, and neither should you! Stay focused, stay determined, and remember—doing your duty with full effort is the real victory!

CHAPTER FOURTEEN

The Summit of Determination

Neha was a young woman who had always been ambitious but never really pushed herself beyond her comfort zone. She worked as a project manager at a fast-paced tech company in the city. Day after day, she juggled meetings, deadlines, and tasks. While she was good at her job, something inside her felt unfulfilled, as if there was more to life than just work.

Her life took an unexpected turn when she was selected to attend an external leadership program. The program promised to push participants out of their comfort zones and encourage them to dream bigger. Neha was excited but also nervous. She wasn't sure if she was ready for the challenges it would bring. But little did she know that one of the speakers would change her life forever.

At the program, Neha was introduced to Bachendri Pal, the first Indian woman to reach the summit of Mount Everest. Bachendri's story left Neha spellbound. As she listened to Bachendri share her journey of perseverance, self-belief, and grit, Neha felt a stirring in her heart. She had always admired strength and resilience but had never thought of applying those qualities to her own life outside of work.

After the session, Neha gathered the courage to approach Bachendri. "Ma'am, your story is incredible. But I don't think I could ever do something like that. I'm not strong enough. I've never even climbed a mountain."

Bachendri smiled, her eyes filled with understanding. "Strength doesn't come from physical power alone. It comes from your mindset. When you set your sights on a goal, the strength you need will appear. The summit you reach isn't just about the mountain, it's about conquering the doubts in your mind. If you're determined, nothing can stop you."

Neha left the conversation feeling inspired. For the first time, she began to think beyond her office job. Could she really aim for something as daring as climbing a mountain?

Weeks passed, and Neha couldn't shake the thought of reaching a summit. She started researching and learning about climbing and mountaineering. One evening, after several weeks of contemplation, she signed up for a basic climbing course. It felt like a huge leap, but something inside her knew that this was the challenge she had been waiting for.

During the course, Neha faced physical challenges she had never imagined. There were days when her muscles ached, and her confidence wavered. She struggled with the steep inclines and the harsh conditions, but she remembered Bachendri's words. *"If you're determined, nothing can stop you."* She kept pushing through, bit by bit, even when it felt like her body wasn't keeping up.

However, it wasn't just physical strength that she had to develop. Neha began to understand the importance of mental perseverance. The journey was long and exhausting, but with each step, she grew stronger in both body and mind. And with each setback, she reminded herself that the only way to fail was by giving up.

A few months into her training, Neha reached out to Bachendri for guidance. She knew that to truly test her limits, she needed expert mentorship. Bachendri welcomed her request and began to guide her through the process of preparing for a summit expedition. Their conversations were often long, with Bachendri providing advice on everything from mental discipline to physical conditioning.

"There will be times when you'll want to stop," Bachendri warned her. "The climb will be difficult, and it will feel like you've reached your limit. But remember, Neha, the summit isn't just about reaching the top. It's about the determination to keep going, step by step."

Neha trained relentlessly, pushing herself harder than she ever thought possible. And when the day finally arrived to attempt her first serious climb, Neha was nervous but determined. The climb was demanding, and there were moments when the altitude made it difficult to breathe, when her legs felt like they would collapse under her. She wanted to stop, to turn around and quit, but she thought of Bachendri's words again.

"The summit isn't just about the mountain, it's about conquering the doubts in your mind."

One step at a time, Neha continued. When she felt like her energy was drained, she reminded herself that the climb wasn't just physical—it was a mental battle. She focused on each step, telling herself that she could do this. And with each step, her confidence grew.

As she neared the summit, Neha felt tears welling up in her eyes. She had come so far. She had doubted herself so many times along the way, but here she was, standing at the top of the mountain, looking out at the world below. She had done it. She had reached the summit, not because she was the strongest climber, but because she had refused to give up.

When Neha returned to the base camp, news of her accomplishment spread quickly. Her colleagues back at work were amazed by her journey. A few days later, her manager approached her with a request.

"Neha, your story has inspired so many of us. Would you be willing to share your experience with the team? I think it would motivate everyone to push past their own limits."

Nervous but excited, Neha agreed. At the company event, she stood in front of a room full of her colleagues. As she recounted her journey, from meeting Bachendri Pal to standing at the summit, she emphasized the lessons she had learned.

"It wasn't just about reaching the top of the mountain," she said, her voice steady. "It was about realizing that perseverance is the most important tool we have. Every step I took, no matter how small, brought me closer to my goal. Success isn't about being the strongest or the fastest. It's about refusing to give up, even when the path is hard."

The room erupted into applause. Neha's words had struck a chord with everyone. Her colleagues left the event not only inspired but also determined to tackle their own challenges with the same persistence Neha had shown.For Neha, the journey to the summit had been life-changing. And now, she realized that her story was helping others find their own strength, one step at a time.

Life lesson: Perseverance is the key to success.

Perseverance is the key to success. No matter how challenging the path, taking one step at a time with determination can lead to incredible achievements.

Bhagavad Gita Shloka :
*'sa niscayena yoktavyo yogo nirvinna-cetasa
sankalpa-prabhavan kamams tyaktva sarvan asesatah
manasaivendriya-gramam viniyamya samantatah'*
(Chapter 6 , Verse 24)

Translation – 'One should engage oneself in the practice of yoga with determination and faith and not be deviated from the path. One should abandon, without exception, all material desires born of mental speculation and thus control all the senses on all sides by the mind.'

Takeaway - Krishna teaches us that perseverance is all about **staying focused on what truly matters and not letting distractions take over.** Imagine sitting down to study, but—ding!—your phone lights up with a message. One quick reply turns into 10 minutes of scrolling, and before you know it, you've lost focus. Sound familiar? **Real perseverance means choosing long-term success over short-term distractions.**

Think of it like training for a big game or competition. Would an athlete stop practicing to check social media every five minutes? No way! They stay focused because they know their goals are bigger than temporary fun. As a student, your "training" is studying, learning, and sharpening your mind. That means putting away distractions, saying "no" to temptations, and giving your best effort—because your future self will thank you!

But perseverance isn't just about staying off your phone—it's also about **staying strong inside.** When school feels tough, when a subject doesn't make sense, or when you feel like giving up—that's when true perseverance kicks in. Instead of quitting, take a deep breath, refocus, and keep going. **Every time you push through a challenge, you build the mental strength and determination that will help you succeed in anything you do.**

The path to success isn't always easy, but **staying disciplined, focused, and determined will take you wherever you want to go.So, are you ready to train your mind like a champion and keep moving forward—no matter what?**

The Unwavering Mother

In the quiet village of Lakshmipur, nestled between rolling fields and dusty roads, lived Kamala, a woman known for her steady strength and warm heart. Life had been a constant challenge for her, but Kamala never let her struggles define her. She believed in one mantra: *"Happiness and sorrow are two sides of the same coin. What matters is how you carry on."*

Kamala had married Ramesh, a carpenter, at a young age. Together, they built a modest life, raising three children—Ravi, Ananya, and Meera. Though Ramesh worked tirelessly, his income was barely enough to make ends meet. Kamala, a housewife, made it her mission to create a loving, nurturing home.

Every morning, Kamala would rise before the sun, lighting the small kerosene stove in their dimly lit kitchen. The aroma of spiced lentils and freshly made chapatis would fill the air as she prepared meals for the family. Some days, there wasn't enough food to go around, and Kamala would quietly eat less, ensuring her children were fed.

"Ma, why aren't you eating more?" little Meera once asked, her voice filled with concern.

Kamala smiled and stroked her daughter's hair. "A mother's hunger disappears when her children are happy," she replied softly.

As the children grew, so did the challenges. Ravi struggled with his studies, often failing in math exams. Ananya had a curious mind but couldn't focus, often losing herself in daydreams. Meera, the youngest, lacked confidence and hesitated to speak up in class.

One day, a neighbor remarked, "Kamala, why do you put in so much effort? Your children aren't exactly shining stars in school."

Kamala's calm face betrayed no irritation. "Every seed takes its own time to sprout," she replied. "My job is to water them and ensure they have the sunlight they need. They will bloom when they're ready."

When Ramesh fell ill, their financial struggles worsened. Kamala didn't flinch. She began taking on odd jobs—stitching clothes, cleaning houses, and even selling handmade pickles at the local market.

Her days stretched endlessly. After finishing her work outside, she would return home to cook, clean, and help her children with their studies. She made learning fun, turning math problems into games for Ravi, quizzing Ananya on general knowledge during chores, and encouraging Meera to read aloud while she worked.

One evening, Ravi threw his textbook onto the floor. "I can't do it, Ma! Math is impossible for me!"

Kamala knelt beside him, picking up the book. "Ravi, do you remember when you learned to ride your bicycle? You fell so many times, but did you stop trying?"

"No," Ravi mumbled, looking at the floor.

"Exactly," Kamala said with a gentle smile. "Math is the same. Every mistake you make is a step toward getting it right. Don't give up, my son. Keep trying."

Her unwavering faith in her children gave them the courage to persevere.

Over the years, Kamala's hard work began to pay off in small ways. Ravi discovered a love for mechanics and started repairing bicycles in the village, earning a little money. Ananya became a natural teacher, helping younger children with their studies. Meera found her voice, surprising everyone with a beautiful speech during a school event.

Despite these small victories, life continued to test Kamala. One harsh winter, their roof began to leak, and the family had to huddle together in a single room to stay warm. Kamala reassured her children, "Every storm passes, and after it, the sun shines brighter. We'll fix this roof together."

And they did.

Years passed, and Kamala's children grew into young adults. Ravi became an engineer, designing and repairing machines. Ananya pursued her passion for teaching and became a school principal. Meera, inspired by her mother's nurturing nature, became a nurse, bringing comfort to those in need.

One evening, as the family gathered in their newly built home in the city, Ravi said, "Ma, do you realize what you've done for us? You taught us that no matter how hard life gets, we should keep going. You never let us feel like we were less, even when others doubted us."

Ananya added, "You taught us that happiness isn't about having everything—it's about finding joy in what we have."

Meera, with tears in her eyes, said, "You gave us strength, Ma. You gave us everything, even when you had so little for yourself."

Kamala's eyes glistened with tears, but her smile was steady. "My children, life is a journey filled with highs and lows. Happiness and sorrow, gain and loss—they are all part of it. What matters is how we face them. Never let success make you arrogant or failure make you lose hope. Keep doing your duty with love and determination. That is the secret to a fulfilling life."

Kamala's story became an inspiration for many in Lakshmipur. Young mothers would come to her for advice, and even elders admired her resilience.

One day, Kamala was invited to speak at the village school. Standing before a crowd of young students and their parents, she said, "Life will test you, but don't let it break you. Treat happiness and sorrow as passing clouds. Focus on your duties, give your best, and trust that your efforts will bear fruit. Remember, it's not what life gives you, but how you respond to it that defines your journey."The audience erupted in applause, and Kamala's children stood proudly, knowing that their mother's lessons had shaped not only their lives but also the lives of everyone who listened.

Life lesson: Remain steadfast.

Happiness and sorrow, gain and loss, are fleeting. True strength lies in treating them alike and performing your duties with unwavering determination and love.

Bhagavad Gita Shloka :
'sukha-duhkhe same krtva labhalabhau jayajayau
tato yuddhaya yujyasva naivam papam avapsyasi'
(Chapter 2 , Verse 38)

Translation – 'Do thou fight for the sake of fighting, without considering happiness or distress, loss or gain, victory or defeat – and by so doing you shall never incur sin.'

Takeaway - Krishna teaches us a powerful life hack—**don't let what happens outside control how you feel inside!Whether you win or lose, succeed or fail, your worth doesn't change.** What really matters is that you give your best effort without stressing too much about the outcome.

Imagine playing your favorite sport. If you focus only on winning, you might feel nervous, make mistakes, or get upset if things don't go your way. But if you focus on playing your best, you'll enjoy the game, improve your skills, and feel good—no matter the result. Life works the same way!

Krishna reminds Arjuna that success and failure, happiness and sadness—these are all temporary. What really counts is how you respond to them. If you let a bad grade, a tough exam, or a small failure ruin your day, you're giving your power away! Instead, **stay**

calm, focused, and keep moving forward.

As a student, this means not freaking out over a tough test or comparing your grades to others. Some days will be great, others not so much—but if you focus on learning instead of just the results, you'll be happier, stress-free, and always improving.

So next time things don't go as planned, **take a deep breath, smile, and remind yourself—your job is to do your best and let go of the rest!**

CHAPTER SIXTEEN

The Blacksmith's Fire

In the quiet village of Suryanagar, a young apprentice named Kunal dreamed of becoming a skilled blacksmith. He admired his teacher, Raghav, whose craftsmanship was unmatched in the region. Raghav's creations—whether sturdy farming tools or delicate ornamental pieces—were renowned for their precision and beauty.

Determined to follow in his mentor's footsteps, Kunal joined the forge with enthusiasm. The initial days were exciting. He loved the roar of the fire, the glow of molten metal, and the ringing sound of the hammer striking the anvil. But as time passed, Kunal's excitement began to wane.

One evening, Kunal sat by the forge, his shoulders slumped in frustration. "Raghav," he began hesitantly, "no matter how hard I try, the metal refuses to bend the way I want. My tools break easily, and nothing I make looks as good as your work."

Raghav set down his hammer and smiled. "Come here, Kunal," he said, beckoning him to the forge.

Taking a dull, unshaped piece of iron, Raghav placed it into the blazing fire. "Watch closely," he instructed. As the metal glowed a fiery red, Raghav pulled it out with his tongs and began striking it rhythmically on the anvil. Sparks flew with every blow, and the iron slowly took shape.

"This fire," Raghav explained, holding up the glowing metal, "is not here to destroy. It's here to prepare the iron for change. Without the fire, the metal remains hard and unyielding. The hammer, too, is not your enemy—it is the tool that brings out the metal's potential."

Kunal furrowed his brow. "But the fire and hammer seem harsh. Isn't the metal in pain?"

Raghav chuckled. "Perhaps, if the metal had feelings, it might think so. But without the fire to soften it and the hammer to shape it, this iron would remain a simple, useless lump. Challenges in life are much the same. They may seem harsh, but they are what prepare and shape us into something better. Growth doesn't come from comfort—it comes from enduring and learning through effort."

Kunal nodded slowly, though doubt still lingered. Could he truly endure the fire and the hammer of his own struggles?

The next morning, Raghav gave Kunal a special task: to forge a strong chisel.

Kunal set to work with determination. He heated the iron until it glowed, then began hammering it. Each strike of the hammer sent sparks flying, and the metal resisted him at first. His arms ached, and sweat dripped down his face, but Raghav's words echoed in his mind: "The fire isn't the enemy—it's the guide."

As the hours passed, Kunal's frustration gave way to focus. He reheated the metal when it cooled too quickly and corrected his mistakes patiently. By the end of the day, he held up a sharp, sturdy chisel. It wasn't flawless, but it was strong—a tool worthy of the forge.

When Kunal presented his work, Raghav inspected it closely. A proud smile spread across his face. "Well done, Kunal. This chisel is more than a tool—it is proof of your perseverance. Remember this: life will bring its own fires and hammers. Face them with determination, and you'll emerge stronger every time."

Months later, Kunal had grown into a confident blacksmith, shaping metal with skill and precision. One day, a young boy named Veer approached him, holding a broken farming tool. "Can you fix this for me?" Veer asked hesitantly.

Kunal nodded and got to work. As he hammered the glowing metal, Veer watched in awe. "Doesn't the fire frighten you?" the boy asked.

Kunal smiled, recalling his own early struggles. "The fire used to seem intimidating," he admitted, "but I've learned it's not something to fear. The fire and hammer are what make the metal strong, just like challenges make us stronger. It's not about avoiding difficulties—it's about using them to grow." Veer listened intently, inspired by Kunal's words.

Life lesson: Face challenges with courage.

Challenges, like the fire and hammer that shape metal, may seem intense, but they are essential for growth. By facing them with courage and determination, we can transform into something stronger and more resilient.

Bhagavad Gita Shloka :
'hato va prapsyasi svargam jitva va bhoksyase mahim tasmad uttistha kaunteya yuddhaya krta-niscayah'
(Chapter 2 , Verse 37)

Translation – 'O son of Kunti, either you will be killed on the battlefield and attain the heavenly planets, or you will conquer and enjoy the earthly kingdom. Therefore, get up with determination and fight.'

Takeaway - Krishna teaches Arjuna an epic truth—no matter what happens, **you grow when you face challenges with courage!** If a warrior wins, they enjoy victory, and if they fall, they reach heaven—either way, they gain something valuable. This shows that **what really matters isn't winning or losing—it's showing up, giving your best, and never backing down.**

Life works the same way! Challenges—like tough exams, competitions, or learning something new—can feel scary at first. But fear fades when you take action! Instead of worrying about failing or stressing over success, focus on giving your 100%. Because here's the secret: **win or lose, you always learn, and that's what makes you stronger!**

Think about a video game. Every time you take on a new level, it's challenging. But if you keep playing, you get better, stronger, and unlock new skills. Life's challenges work the same way! **Each problem is a chance to level up.**

True courage isn't about never feeling scared—it's about showing up even when things feel tough. So, next time you face a challenge, stand tall like a warrior, take a deep breath, and go for it. Because **no matter the outcome, you're already winning by trying!**

CHAPTER SEVENTEEN

The Roller Coaster Ride

Samar and his best friend Ravi stood at the entrance of the amusement park, gazing up at the giant roller coaster towering above them. It was the newest and most thrilling ride in the park, with steep drops, sharp twists, and a massive loop that seemed to defy gravity. Samar's eyes sparkled with excitement, while Ravi's face turned pale.

"I don't know about this, Samar," Ravi muttered, clutching his backpack nervously. "What if I can't handle it? What if it's too much?"

Samar chuckled, nudging him playfully. "Come on, Ravi! It's just a ride. It's not forever, you know. It's like life—there are ups, downs, and crazy twists, but it all passes. You just have to hang on and enjoy it while it lasts."

Ravi sighed, looking at the screaming riders whizzing by. "But what if I hate it? What if it doesn't stop?"

Samar put a reassuring hand on his friend's shoulder. "Nothing lasts forever—not the scary parts, not the fun parts. It's just a moment. Trust me, you'll be fine."

Reluctantly, Ravi followed Samar into the line for the coaster. The closer they got to the front, the louder Ravi's heart pounded. He watched as riders ahead were strapped into their seats, their nervous laughter blending with the excited screams of those already on the ride.

When their turn came, Ravi hesitated. "Maybe I should just wait for you at the exit," he said, his voice trembling.

Samar grinned and pulled him toward the seat. "No way! You've got this, Ravi. Just breathe and trust the process. It's all part of the experience."

As the safety bar clicked into place, Ravi gripped it tightly, his knuckles turning white. The ride began to climb, the rhythmic clanking of the chain pulling them higher and higher.

As they reached the top, Ravi's eyes widened at the sight of the park sprawled out below them. The coaster paused for a brief moment before plunging down at breakneck speed. Ravi screamed, his stomach flipping, but Samar's laughter cut through the wind.

"See, Ravi?" Samar shouted over the rush of air. "It's wild, but it's amazing!"

The ride twisted and turned, throwing them upside down and sideways. At times, Ravi felt like he couldn't breathe, and at others, he found himself laughing uncontrollably. By the time the ride slowed to a stop, Ravi's heart was racing, but a huge smile was plastered across his face.

"I did it!" he exclaimed, stepping off the coaster with wobbly legs. "I can't believe I actually did it!"

Samar gave him a high-five. "I told you! It's all about hanging on and knowing it'll end. Life's the same way—nothing is permanent, so you might as well enjoy the ride while it lasts."

As they walked through the park, Ravi thought about Samar's words. He realized that his fear hadn't been about the ride itself but about the uncertainty of the experience. Yet, by facing it, he discovered something important—challenges, no matter how daunting, were always temporary.

Later that evening, as they sat by the park fountain, Ravi turned to Samar. "You know, you were right. Life really is like a roller coaster. The scary parts don't last forever, and neither do the good parts. But when you accept that, it makes everything feel more meaningful."Samar smiled, throwing an arm around his friend. "Exactly, Ravi. So, the next time life gets a little bumpy, just remember this day. You've already conquered the scariest coaster in the park—what's stopping you from taking on anything else?"

Life lesson: Nothing is permanent.

Life is full of ups, downs, twists, and turns, just like a roller coaster. The key is to embrace the experience, knowing that nothing is permanent. Both the challenges and the joys will pass, so face each moment with courage and determination.

Bhagavad Gita Shloka :
'matra-sparsas tu kaunteya sitosna-sukha-duhkha-dah
agamapayino nityas tams titiksasva bharata'
(Chapter 2 , Verse 14)

Translation – 'O son of Kunti, the non-permanent appearance of happiness and distress and their disappearance in due course are like the appearance and disappearance of winter and summer seasons. They arise from sense perception, O scion of Bharata and one must learn to tolerate them without them being disturbed.'

Takeaway - Krishna teaches us an awesome life hack—**nothing lasts forever! Just like summer turns into winter and day fades into night, both happy and tough times come and go.So,if you're feeling down, remember—it won't last forever. And if you're riding high on success, enjoy it, but don't get too attached—because that, too, will change.** The key? Stay calm, stay steady, and keep going!

Think of life like surfing on ocean waves. Some waves lift you up, and some pull you down, but if you learn to balance and ride with confidence, you'll always move forward. If you panic when a big wave comes, you'll wipe out! But if you stay focused and flexible, you'll handle whatever comes your way.

Whether it's acing a test or struggling with a tough subject, don't let success make you lazy or failure make you quit. Both are just moments—they don't define you! What really matters is your effort, determination, and ability to adapt.

So next time life throws a challenge at you, take a deep breath and ride the wave. Because Krishna reminds us—**strong minds don't break with the tides; they rise with them!**

CHAPTER EIGHTEEN

The Wandering Kite

Meera lived in a bustling city filled with tall buildings, honking cars, and endless chatter. Her apartment balcony overlooked a small park, one of the few open spaces in her neighborhood. One Saturday, her father surprised her with a vibrant red-and-yellow kite.

"A kite? In the city?" Meera asked, tilting her head.

Her father smiled. "Even cities have skies, Meera. Let's take it to the park and give it a try."

Excited but uncertain, Meera followed him to the park. The playground was filled with children, joggers ran along the paths, and a group of older kids were flying kites high above the trees. The sight of those kites weaving through the air filled her with excitement, but also nervousness.

Her father helped her set up the kite. "Hold the string tightly," he instructed. As she released the kite into the air, the wind caught it, and for a moment, it soared. But as soon as a strong gust came, the kite spiraled wildly and crashed into the ground.

Meera groaned. "This isn't working! The wind here is too unpredictable. I'll never get it right."

Her father knelt beside her, picking up the kite. "Flying a kite isn't about controlling the wind, Meera. It's about understanding it. The kite is like your mind—it's restless and gets pulled in all directions. You don't fight the wind; you guide the kite gently back on track."

Meera frowned. "But it's so frustrating when it doesn't go where I want!"

Her father chuckled. "That's because you're trying to control it too much. Let's try again, and this time, stay calm and steady, even when it feels difficult."

Every evening after school, Meera and her father went to the park. At first, her kite continued to spiral and dive, and she often felt like giving up. The wind between the buildings was unpredictable, changing direction without warning.

"Feel the tension in the string," her father would say. "When the wind pulls hard, don't jerk it. Hold steady and gently guide it back."

Meera began to notice the patterns of the wind. She learned to adjust her movements, letting the kite dance with the breeze instead of fighting against it. One evening, after weeks of practice, her kite soared higher than ever before, gliding gracefully above the park.

"I did it, Papa!" Meera exclaimed, her face glowing with pride.

Her father smiled. "Yes, you did. And just like the kite, your mind can soar when you learn to guide it with patience and care."

As days passed, Meera started noticing how her thoughts were often like her kite—pulling her in different directions. When she felt overwhelmed by schoolwork or annoyed by noisy neighbors, her mind seemed to spiral out of control.

One day, after a long day at school, Meera came home to find her father sitting in their small living room, eyes closed, sitting in a calm posture. He was meditating, something he did every evening. Intrigued, Meera quietly sat down beside him.

"Dad, what are you doing?" she asked softly.

Her father opened one eye and smiled gently. "I'm meditating, Meera. It's a way to calm my mind and find peace. In the world we live in, our thoughts can be like a kite in the wind—uncontrolled and scattered. But through meditation, we can learn to guide them, just like we guide a kite."

Meera looked at him, her curiosity piqued. "But how does sitting still help with that? My mind is always racing."

Her father chuckled. "It's like flying a kite. At first, it's hard to control. The wind pulls it in different directions, and the string gets tangled. But with practice, you learn to guide the kite gently, and the wind no longer controls it. The same is true for the mind. Meditation teaches us to bring the mind back when it starts to wander, to focus on one thing at a time, and to calm our thoughts."

One day, while struggling with a particularly difficult math problem, Meera put down her pencil and closed her eyes. She took a deep breath and whispered to herself, "Bring it back, like the kite." Slowly, her frustration faded, and she was able to focus again.

Her father noticed her calm demeanor and said, "You're learning an important lesson, When your mind wanders, you gently bring it back. Try meditation, it will help you find peace, even in the chaos of city life."

Meera wasn't sure how sitting quietly would help, but she decided to give it a try. Her father guided her through a simple meditation: she closed her eyes, focused on her breath, and tried to keep her thoughts from drifting. At first, her mind raced with thoughts about school, her friends, and the upcoming weekend plans. But slowly, she remembered her father's words and gently brought her focus back to her breathing.

The next day, Meera decided to meditate every morning before school. She made it a part of her routine, starting with just five minutes, but over time, it helped her feel more centered and less distracted throughout the day. When she sat down to study, her thoughts no longer jumped from one thing to the next, and when she spoke with her friends, she listened more attentively.

One afternoon, when Meera was flying her kite in the park, she noticed something different. As she steadied the kite, guiding it through the wind, she found that her mind, too, felt calmer. She realized that the practice of meditation had helped her learn how to be present, to focus, and to remain steady in the midst of the stormy thoughts that used to take her off course. The more she practiced meditation, the more her mind felt like the kite—gently guided by her own steady hands rather than tossed around by the wind.

Later that day, her cousin Aarav came over, eager to learn how to fly a kite. As they worked together, Aarav struggled, his kite swerving uncontrollably in the wind. Meera smiled, remembering how she had once felt the same way. "Aarav, it's just like meditation," she said. "Sometimes, the kite will drift away, but if you gently guide it back, it will soar."

Together, they worked on flying his kite. After several tries, Aarav's kite finally took off, wobbling at first, but soon soaring gracefully alongside Meera's. Aarav's eyes widened in delight as he watched the kite climb higher, the tail fluttering in the breeze. A wide grin spread across his face, and his laughter echoed through the park like music. He looked up at his cousin, Meera, with a sparkle in his eyes, full of admiration. "I did it, Meera! I really did it!" he shouted, his voice filled with pride.

Meera smiled back at him, her heart swelling with happiness. Aarav's joy was her reward. As the two of them stood there, watching their kites dance in the sky, Meera realized that meditation, like the kite, had taught her to guide her thoughts and emotions, to remain grounded, and to face life's challenges with calm and clarity.She knew that as she continued to practice meditation, her mind would become even steadier, and just like a kite soaring high in the sky, she too would rise above life's distractions, finding peace and balance in the midst of the storm.

Life lesson: Meditate daily.

Just like a kite in the wind, the mind can be restless, but through meditation, we can learn to gently guide it back to focus and calm. Meditation helps us stay grounded, find clarity, and face challenges with a peaceful mind.

Bhagavad Gita Shloka :
*'yato yato niscalati manas cancalam asthiram
tatas tato niyamyaitad atmany eva vasam nayet'*
(Chapter 6 , Verse 26)

Translation – 'From wherever the mind wanders due to its flickering and unsteady nature, one must certainly withdraw it and bring it back under the control of the self.'

Takeaway - Ever feel like your mind is a monkey jumping from branch to branch? One second you're thinking about school, the next about your favorite game, then about what's for dinner! Krishna teaches us that **meditation is like a secret training ground for your mind—helping you stay focused, calm, and in control.**

Think of meditation like leveling up in a game —the more you practice, the stronger your mind becomes! At first, sitting still might feel impossible, but just like learning a new skill, it gets easier over time. Meditation isn't about stopping your thoughts—it's about learning to guide them, like steering a ship through waves.

But here's the coolest part—**meditation helps you see who you really are! You're not just your thoughts, your worries, or what others expect from you. Deep inside, you are strong, calm, and limitless.** Meditation helps you break free from stress, self-doubt, and negativity, replacing them with confidence, clarity, and peace.

And guess what? You don't have to be a monk on a mountain to meditate! Just a few minutes each day—focusing on your breath, a calming mantra, or even just quiet reflection—can help you stay cool during tough moments, handle stress like a pro, and stay focused on what really matters.

So, are you ready to unlock your inner superpower? **Start today, one breath at a time!**

CHAPTER NINETEEN

Arun's Journey to Fulfillment

Arun had always been laser-focused on his career. From the moment he graduated from college, he had set his sights on climbing the corporate ladder. Every day, he worked tirelessly, often staying late at the office and sacrificing his personal time for work. Promotions came one after another, and the money piled up, but despite all his success, a nagging feeling of emptiness lingered in his heart. He had everything he thought he wanted, but somehow, he felt as if something was missing.

One afternoon, after a particularly long week of meetings and deadlines, Arun decided to meet Priya, an old friend from college. She was someone who always radiated positivity, and Arun couldn't help but notice how content and happy she seemed. They sat at a café, sipping their coffee, and after a few moments of catching up, Arun couldn't contain his curiosity any longer.

"Priya," he asked, "You always seem so happy. What's your secret?"

Priya smiled, her eyes sparkling with warmth. "It's not a secret, Arun," she said, "I volunteer at the local charity. It's been the most fulfilling part of my life. Helping others, especially children who don't have as much as we do, brings me so much joy. It's amazing how giving without expecting anything in return can make you feel truly rich."

Arun raised an eyebrow. "Volunteering? I don't have time for that. My job is my priority. My career is where I can make a difference."

Priya's smile didn't falter, but she simply said, "Maybe one day, you'll see that making a difference doesn't just mean in the boardroom. Sometimes, the real impact is made outside of work."

A week later, Arun visited his grandmother, a wise woman who had always been his source of advice. He confessed to her what he had been feeling. "Grandma, I'm successful, but I don't feel fulfilled. I'm always chasing the next promotion, but no matter how much I achieve, I never feel truly happy. I thought that success would bring me contentment, but it hasn't."

His grandmother, who had always lived with a deep sense of peace and kindness, looked at him with a soft smile. "Arun, true happiness isn't found in what you receive. It's found in what you give. You've been so focused on climbing the ladder, but perhaps it's time to ask yourself—what are you doing to lift others along the way? Happiness and fulfillment come from selfless service to others, not from selfish gain."

Arun felt a stirring inside of him. Could it really be that simple? His grandmother's words stayed with him, and the next time he saw Priya, he decided to take the plunge. "I want to try volunteering," he said, "I want to see if it really makes a difference."

Priya's face lit up with excitement. "That's wonderful, Arun! You won't regret it."

The following weekend, Arun visited the charity for the first time. It wasn't an extravagant organization, but it was warm and welcoming. There were children in need of mentorship, seniors looking for companionship, and families struggling to make ends meet. Arun initially felt out of place, unsure of what to do or how to help, but he decided to jump in anyway.

At first, the work seemed small—helping kids with their homework, sorting donations, or just listening to someone's story. But as the days passed, Arun began to notice something that he hadn't expected: a deep sense of fulfillment. Every time he saw the smile of a child who had learned something new, every time he held the hand of an elderly person who felt lonely, Arun felt a sense of purpose he had never felt before.

One evening, after spending time with a group of children, Arun walked out of the center and paused. The sun was setting, painting the sky with warm oranges and purples, and he felt a sense of peace wash over him that he hadn't experienced in years. For the first time in a long time, he felt truly content.

As the weeks passed, Arun continued volunteering, and his sense of purpose only grew stronger. He realized that giving his time and energy to others had filled a void he didn't even know existed. His work at the charity didn't diminish his professional success; instead, it enriched his life in ways that his career never could. He had learned that the true measure of success wasn't just in promotions or financial gain—it was in how much you gave to the world around you.

One evening, as he was helping a group of children with a school project, one of the kids looked up at him and said, "Arun Uncle, you're always helping us. Why do you do it?"

Arun smiled, feeling a warmth in his chest. "Because it makes me happy," he said. "Seeing you all happy, learning new things, or just having someone to talk to—makes me realize that giving is the best thing I can do. It fills my heart with joy."

The child smiled back, "You're like a superhero, Arun Uncle, but without a cape!"

Arun laughed, feeling his heart swell with pride. "Maybe, just maybe, we all have the power to be heroes. We just need to choose to help others."As he continued his journey of giving, Arun found not just a sense of purpose, but also a deep connection with the people around him. His relationship with Priya became even stronger as they worked together to make the world a better place. They organized fundraisers, collected donations, and mentored young people, and through it all, Arun felt more alive and fulfilled than ever.

Life lesson: Work for the welfare of the world.

True happiness comes not from what we gain, but from what we give. Selfless service to others brings fulfillment, joy, and a sense of purpose, enriching our lives in ways that material success cannot. Through helping others, we find our true calling.

Bhagavad Gita Shloka :
'saktah karmany avidvamso yatha kurvanti bharata
kuryad vidvams tathasaktas cikirsur loka-sangraham'
(Chapter 3 , Verse 25)

Translation – 'As the ignorant perform their duties with attachment to results, the learned may similarly act, but without attachment, for the sake of leading people on the right path.'

Takeaway - Krishna teaches us an amazing secret—the happiest people aren't the ones who only think about themselves. Instead, true joy comes from helping others without expecting anything in return!

Think about it—have you ever helped a friend with homework, made someone smile, or shared your lunch with someone who forgot theirs? Didn't it feel awesome? That's because **selfless actions create real happiness! When you do things just for personal gain, you might feel good for a while, but when you help others with love, you feel something even deeper—real satisfaction.**

Krishna reminds us that the wisest people work for the good of everyone, not just themselves. They inspire others by leading with kindness and showing that success isn't just about what you get, but about what you give. **Work done with love, without selfishness, is like a form of worship—it brings people together, makes the world better, and helps you grow as a person.**

So, what can you do? Lend a hand, share, support, and be kind—not because you have to, but because you can. Whether it's helping a friend, caring for animals, or doing small acts of kindness, every selfless action creates ripples of positivity.

Being a hero doesn't mean wearing a cape—it means lifting others up, spreading kindness, and making the world brighter, one good deed at a time. So, are you ready to be a hero today?

CHAPTER TWENTY

The Little Lantern of Faith

In a small town nestled at the edge of the mountains, there lived a young girl named Aisha. She was known for her bright smile and endless curiosity. Aisha loved exploring the fields and the forests that surrounded her village, but more than anything, she loved listening to the stories her grandmother would tell her every evening.

Grandmother's stories were filled with wisdom—stories about courage, kindness, and faith in God. Aisha had grown up hearing about how faith could move mountains, how prayers could heal hearts, and how God's guidance was always present, even when it felt like the world was dark.

One evening, as they sat under the stars, Aisha turned to her grandmother and asked, "Grandma, why do we need to remember God all the time? Doesn't it feel like we should rely on ourselves sometimes?"

Her grandmother, a woman of deep faith and experience, smiled softly. "Ah, my dear, that's a good question. Let me tell you a story."

Aisha listened closely, eager for another lesson wrapped in a tale.

"Many years ago, there was a small village that was often shrouded in mist. The villagers could hardly see beyond their homes, and the roads were so dark that even the bravest traveler could easily lose their way. In this village, there was a young boy named Raghav. He was always busy—he worked hard on the farm, helped his family with chores, and played with his friends. But there was one thing Raghav never seemed to do: He never prayed. He believed that as long as he worked hard, he could solve all his problems."

Aisha sat up, intrigued by the story. "So, what happened to Raghav?"

Her grandmother continued, "One day, a terrible storm swept through the village. The winds howled, the trees shook, and the river began to flood. Raghav's family home was in danger of being washed away, and everyone was scared. Raghav tried his best to fix things—he tied up ropes, built barriers, and worked until his hands bled. But in the end, the storm was too powerful. His efforts weren't enough."

Aisha's eyes widened. "Oh no, what did Raghav do?"

Her grandmother's eyes sparkled as she continued, "In the midst of all the chaos, Raghav suddenly remembered something his grandmother had once told him: 'When you are lost and helpless, remember God. Just like a lantern lights the path in darkness, God's guidance can light your way when things seem impossible.'

In that moment, Raghav dropped to his knees and said a simple prayer. He didn't ask for anything grand. He simply said, 'God, please help me find a way.' And do you know what happened, Aisha?"

Aisha shook her head, eager to know.

"Within minutes, the rain stopped. The winds calmed. And when Raghav opened his eyes, he noticed a path leading up the hill that wasn't there before. He quickly grabbed his family and led them to safety. That night, the storm passed, and Raghav's family was safe."

Aisha's heart raced with excitement. "So, it was God who helped Raghav?"

Her grandmother nodded. "Yes, but not just God. It was Raghav's faith in God that opened his heart to finding the solution. Even though he had worked hard, it was in his moment of surrender, when he remembered God, that the way became clear. Sometimes, when we are overwhelmed by life, we forget that we are not alone. Just as a lantern lights the way in the darkest of nights, God's presence can guide us when we remember Him."

Aisha thought for a moment. "But what if I forget to pray? What if I don't know what to say?"

Her grandmother smiled warmly, her voice soft and reassuring. "It's not always about the perfect words, my dear. God listens to the intentions of your heart. Even when you feel lost or confused, just remember to pause and say, 'God, I trust you.' That simple faith is like a light shining in the dark. No matter what happens, when you carry God's presence in your heart, you will never truly be lost."

The next day, Aisha faced a challenge of her own. She had to give a presentation at school in front of all her classmates. She felt nervous, and the thought of speaking in front of so many people made her stomach turn. She remembered her grandmother's words and closed her eyes for a moment.

"God, please help me. Please guide me," she whispered.

When it was her turn to speak, Aisha took a deep breath. The nerves were still there, but as she started talking, she felt a sense of peace wash over her. Her words flowed more easily than she had imagined, and when she finished, her classmates clapped for her. Aisha felt a warm glow in her chest, knowing that it wasn't just her doing the talking—it was God guiding her through the moment.

Later that evening, as Aisha sat with her grandmother, she shared the story of her day. "Grandma, you were right. Remembering God really helped me today. I felt so much more confident after I prayed."

Her grandmother smiled. "I'm proud of you, Aisha. Remembering God doesn't mean that all challenges will vanish, but it helps you face them with peace. When you trust in God and remember that He is always with you, you will never feel alone, no matter how difficult things seem."Aisha hugged her grandmother tightly. "Thank you for teaching me, Grandma. I will always remember God, no matter what."

<u>Life lesson: Always remember God.</u>

Life may bring challenges and moments of uncertainty, but when we remember God, even in our smallest acts, he lights the way for us. True peace comes not from relying solely on ourselves, but in trusting that God is with us every step of the way. Always remember God, and he will guide you through life's darkest moments.

Bhagavad Gita Shloka :
<u>'tasmat sarvesu kalesu mam anusmara yudhya ca</u>
<u>mayy arpita-mano-buddhir mam evaisyasy asamsayah'</u>
(Chapter 8 , Verse 7)

Translation – 'Therefore you should always think of Me in the form of Krishna and at the same time carry out your prescribed duty of fighting. With your activities dedicated to Me and your mind and intelligence fixed on Me, you will attain Me without doubt.'

Takeaway - Krishna teaches Arjuna a powerful truth—being spiritual doesn't mean running away from responsibilities! In fact, it's about doing your best in everything while staying connected to a bigger purpose. Arjuna's duty was to fight in battle, and yours, as a student, is to study, learn, and grow. But here's the cool part—when you see your studies as part of a bigger journey, they stop feeling like a burden and start feeling like a mission!

Think about it—when you give your 100% to something with focus and dedication, whether it's an exam, a project, or even a simple task, you're not just doing it for grades. You're shaping your future! Instead of stressing over results, trust that every effort you put in is helping you grow.

But here's another important lesson—you are never alone in this journey. Life will bring challenges, difficult moments, and times when things feel uncertain. But when you remember God, even in your smallest acts, He lights the way for you. **True peace doesn't come from relying only on yourself, but in trusting that God is walking beside you every step of the way.**

Spirituality isn't just about praying or meditating—it's about bringing mindfulness into everything you do and knowing that **no matter how tough things get, you have a divine guide leading you forward.** When challenges come up (and they always do!), face them with confidence, knowing they're temporary and will only make you stronger.

So next time you open your books, don't see it as just another assignment—see it as a step toward something greater. Stay calm, stay present, and stay focused. **And most importantly, always remember God. Because when you do, He will guide you through life's darkest moments, turning every challenge into an opportunity and every effort into a step toward success.**

"May the wisdom of the Bhagavad Gita guide you, inspire you, and empower you to face life's challenges with courage, compassion, and unwavering belief in yourself. Remember, the journey of growth begins with one small step – so take it, and walk with purpose towards your brightest future."

Jai Shri Krishna